Kate and Roger Johnson are leading treasure hunting experts. Kate Johnson is well known and respected in the field of treasure hunting as both a writer and an experienced practitioner. Her programmatic approach to the hobby has won considerable acclaim in the treasure hunting press. Roger Johnson has worked in the metal detecting industry since its origin in Britain. For a number of years he was Public Relations Officer for Europe's largest manufacturer of treasure hunting equipment, and he now regularly lectures to clubs and societies on all aspects of the hobby.

Kate Johnson

The Complete Book of
TREASURE HUNTING

Photographs by Roger Johnson

A MAYFLOWER BOOK

GRANADA
London Toronto Sydney New York

Published by Granada Publishing Limited in 1981

ISBN 0 583 13420 3

First published in Great Britain by
Arthur Barker Limited 1980
Copyright © Kate Johnson 1980

Granada Publishing Limited
Frogmore, St Albans, Herts AL2 2NF
and
3 Upper James Street, London W1R 4BP
866 United Nations Plaza, New York, NY10017, USA
117 York Street, Sydney, NSW 2000, Australia
100 Skyway Avenue, Rexdale, Ontario, M9W 3A6, Canada
PO Box 84165, Greenside, 2034 Johannesburg, South Africa
61 Beach Road, Auckland, New Zealand

Printed and bound in Great Britain by
Cox and Wyman Ltd, Reading
Phototypesetting by Georgia Origination, Liverpool
Set in Plantin

Granada ®
Granada Publishing ®

CONTENTS

ACKNOWLEDGEMENTS

Special thanks must be made to John Hilton of Manchester Minerals and Don Pople for their kind assistance in compiling the lapidary section, and also to C-Scope Metal Detectors (UK) Limited for the provision of photographs and general assistance.

Apart from those pictures taken specially for the book by Roger Johnson, we are grateful to the following for permission to reproduce photographs:

British Museum: 180 *below*
C-Scope Metal Detectors (UK) Limited: 13 *below*, 18 *below*, 25, 28 *below*, 43, 101 *below*, 125, 134 *above*
Stan Harrison: 105 *below*
Malcolm Hill: 119 *above*
Mr Mayes: 143 *above*

To our son Jamie – a real treasure

1

THE HOBBY

It is an inherent trait of man that he should search for knowledge, and attention is increasingly being focused towards the mysteries of man's distant ancestry and that of the world's antiquities. The artistic charm and ingenuity of artefacts from past civilizations up to the last century lend an educational and pleasing contrast to modern technology.

Countless novels and films have surrounded the discovery of treasure and stories such as Atlantis, Eldorado and Treasure Island have entertained millions and lured them to the romance of buried treasure. Although Britain is not everyone's idea of a treasure island, it cannot be denied that an ever-increasing quantity of spectacular treasures have been discovered all over the country. Until only a few years ago, it was farm workers and building contractors who topped the bill as treasure discoverers, but since the hobby of treasure hunting became popular in Britain, and especially with the introduction of the now familiar metal detector, it is the hobbyists who are responsible for the vast majority of discoveries. It is not rustic sea-chests festooned with riches that the treasure hunter quests, but the astounding number of coin hoards and other treasures which were secreted by our ancestors in periods of unrest, and such discoveries are rarely out of the press for long. The disruption which was caused by such events as the invasions of the Romans, the Danes and the

Normans, or the Wars of the Roses, the civil wars and the Dissolution of the Monasteries, are all instances when Britain would have been a vast repository for buried wealth, a great amount of which was never to be collected.

METAL DETECTING

One of the first treasures discovered with a metal detector was by Barrie Thompson which consisted of some two hundred Anglo-Saxon scettas and realized a value of about £25,000. Treasure hoards such as this continue to be discovered by professional and amateur treasure hunters alike. The largest hoard ever discovered in this country by metal detector users was unearthed near Marlborough in Wiltshire by John Booth and Peter Humphries who had only recently embarked upon the hobby. The hoards consisted of 56,500 third-century double Denarius pieces concealed in a large earthenware pot.

Inspired by such discoveries, three thousand people every month purchase metal detectors and commence an absorbing, educational and lucrative treasure trail of their own. It has been proved on a number of occasions that one does not have to possess the world's best metal detector to reap the rewards of success, for it is the skill used by the operator and the ability to research sites which is of paramount importance. A metal detector costing £25 was, for instance, responsible for the discovery of a treasure hoard worth about £20,000. This treasure, which consisted of nearly three thousand Roman silver and bronze coins, was found on farmland near Lincoln by Mrs Dorothy Harrison and her son-in-law Arthur Greensmith after they investigated a report by a farmer that evidence of Roman pottery had been discovered when ploughing. After obtaining permission from the farmer to search his land and striking an agreement that in the event of a valuable discovery the proceeds would be equally shared, their search commenced. For a few weeks, they searched in their spare time, taking care not to interfere with the farmer's crops,

Bruce Pascoe and the objects collected over one year which won him the
award of Treasure Hunter of the Year 1978.

LEFT: front and back of denarius of Faustina I deified, AD 140.
RIGHT: front and back of denarius of Antonius Pius, AD 159-60.

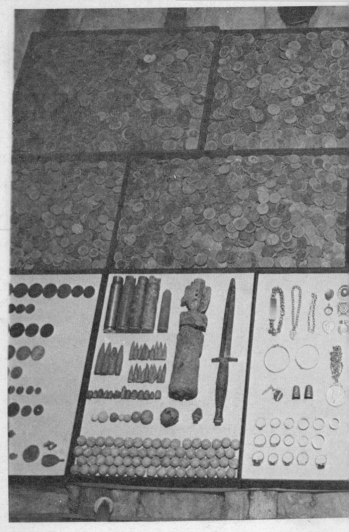

Alex Page's extensive collection shows the variety and range of discoveries that can be made with the use of a metal detector.

with only a few encouraging finds to substantiate their beliefs. But it was not long before their patience and determination were rewarded by the signal which led to the discovery of the Roman pot containing the coins. With the aid of the rest of the family, all the coins inside the pot, and those which had been scattered around the area through ploughing, were retrieved by nightfall and the remainder of that night was spent excitedly counting and identifying the coins. The hoard was promptly reported to the police the next day and the good news was passed on to the farmer. As is compulsory with discoveries of gold or silver, a treasure trove inquest followed to decide whether the hoard was treasure trove and thus the property of the Crown (in which case the finder receives the full market value), or whether it was the property of the finder to use as he wishes. In the case of this Roman hoard, the verdict of the court was given as treasure trove and the coins were passed to the British Museum to decide which coins they wished to purchase from the finders. The proceeds were shared equally, as promised, with the farmer.

In addition to the many spectacular treasure hoards which have been unearthed by metal detector users, encouragement to the novice treasure hunter may also be found in the astounding amount of lost treasures in Britain, as opposed to those which have been deliberately buried. A survey undertaken by the Central Statistics Office only a few years ago estimated that 150 million coins are lost each year in Britain alone, with a value of nearly £3 million. It is also estimated that gold and silver jewellery totalling at least £2 million in value is lost each year. These figures are soon justified, and could even be considered a conservative estimate, by the treasure hunter who employs his metal detector on public areas such as beaches or fairground sites. The extensive collection made by Bruce Pascoe was achieved within only one year of purchasing his metal detector, during which time he spent approximately three hundred hours searching the farmland on which he lives. In addition to the collection of diverse objects made by Alex Page over three years, he has discovered £82 of spendable coinage.

It soon becomes apparent that valuables of the past were just as vulnerable to loss as they are today and the treasure hunter is therefore quite likely to achieve as many ancient objects in his collection as modern. Mr Holbrook of Kent recently discovered a beautiful silver-gilt Anglo-Saxon brooch, decorated with garnets and believed to be of sixth-century origin. The brooch was valued at £1,000 because of its rarity and remarkably well-preserved appearance.

BEACHCOMBING

Many years before the introduction of the metal detector, however, the art of treasure hunting was being successfully used on the beaches of every coastline to provide a means of survival and is, of course, well known as the art of beach-combing. These ancient skills and techniques are being discovered once again by treasure hunters, with or without a metal detector, who are enticed by the healthy atmosphere and the fascination and rewards of this hobby. It is a fact that, even today, people are abandoning former ambitions and aspirations to comb the beach of the treasures it possesses. A lifetime of learning may be made of the sea's habits, studying such features as tides and currents, direction and force of wind, and the layout and history of the coast, all in relation to the distribution of treasures. As expertise increases, so the beach-comber will know the locations of the valuables the sea has deposited. He will know, for instance, where perhaps gold coins will turn up after stormy seas have dislodged them from an ancient shipwreck, or where the summertime tourist losses will occur, depending upon weather conditions and the time of year. An example may be made of Mr Welford who, since childhood, has been involved in seeking the sea's treasures, from earning his pocket-money by shrimping in the rock pools

ABOVE: An Anglo-Saxon brooch made of silver gilt and decorated with garnets, discovered in Kent.

BELOW: The Welford family and the sovereigns picked up while beachcombing on the Kentish coast.

to harvesting the seaside industry's stock of coins and other valuable artefacts. On his local Kentish beach, he has also discovered that certain weather conditions often provide gold sovereigns in one precise area. Because of the consistency of their appearance on the beach according to weather conditions, and owing to the fact that the sovereigns which he has already found are of similar age, an unknown shipwreck out at sea is almost certainly the cause of his frequent finds.

The beauty of beachcombing is that no luck or expensive equipment is necessary, for rewards are a direct result of one's knowledge of the sea and keenness of eye; when this awareness has been developed, the beach will remain forever fruitful to the enlightened beachcomber. No two beaches are alike in their distributions of treasures and one beach is seldom the same on any two days. The basic rules and hints which are outlined in detail in Chapter 2 may be applied on every beach due to the sea's constancy of movement, but success is only achieved when this knowledge is accompanied by careful observation and dedication.

DUMP DIGGING

Another enthralling and educational aspect of treasure hunting may be found in what has popularly become known as 'dump digging' and a visit to an auction which deals in the numerous items which may be collected in this way will prove that it has the added bonus of being an extremely lucrative sideline. It is not uncommon for a rare bottle to fetch £200 or more at auction whilst Victorian ceramic pot lids can command prices of anything between £2 and £500. Yesterday's throwaways are often today's valuables and any item, from a clay pipe to a spare doll's limb, has a price and, almost inevitably, a buyer.

When a productive site has been discovered, results are rapid and an attractive collection soon evolves. Old bottles are amongst the more common spoils but awaiting discovery are other items such as clay pipes, pots and pot lids, vases, figurines, Victorian dolls and a great deal of other household equipment like flat-irons, ceramic bed-warming bottles, antique baby feeders and so on. One never has to look far for an old dumping ground, for on the outskirts of every town and village at least one site would have been utilized for this purpose.

Don Pople, while spending his leisure time in various other treasure hunting activities, has been a keen dump digger for five years. Don has been equally successful in rockhouding and such is the extent of the finds which he has made since he began searching his local beach at Sheerness in Kent in 1962, that the proceeds of the sale of his finds enabled him to pay the deposit on his first house.

ROCKHOUNDING
Rockhounding in Britain is not the limited field which one may first imagine, for both precious and semiprecious stones may be found in rock or pebble form in many parts of the country. Rocks and minerals which may be found in pebble form include rubies, sapphires, gold, silver and even diamonds. From Britain's beaches, rivers and on dry land too, collections may be made of the various quartz and agate families – cornelian, garnet, serpentine, topaz, emerald, sapphire and many more. Methods are given in later chapters for the recognition of such rocks and pebbles in their dull and insignificant appearance and for their transformation by polishing into beautiful gems either for a collection or for jewellery making.

PROSPECTING
Prospecting for gold may also be successfully achieved in Britain, and in nearly every other part of the world. This may at first come as a surprise to some, who immediately associate prospecting with stories of the Wild West of the Klondike gold rush, but it is a fact that Britain too had its gold rush days. In

1502 a gold nugget weighing thirty-five ounces was on one occasion discovered and panning for gold, especially in Scotland, still continues. It has been found by many prospectors, while panning for gold in dry areas such as disused gold mines, that panning can be successfully combined with the use of a metal detector. It must be remembered that in the

Don Pople with a selection of rare glass and pottery collected over five years of dump digging.

Examples of gems which may be found in Britain. *Above left* Mexican potato stone; *above right* amethyst; *centre left* smoky quartz; *below left* quartz crystal; *below right* blue lace agate.

days when these old mines were being worked, sight alone, often in poor lighting, was used as the method of discovery and consequently a great deal of gold went undiscovered and often found its way to the spoil heaps nearby. It is in this manner that both amateur and professional prospectors of the present gold rush in Australia are literally making their fortunes in gold. A forty-seven ounce nugget recently discovered by one prospector was valued at £4,200 for its bullion and £15,000 as a specimen.

All these aspects of treasure hunting, in addition to the ancient art of dowsing for treasure, are explained in detail for anyone to achieve successfully. With the rising concern and necessity for a healthy outdoor activity combined with light physical exercise, no better hobby can be undertaken for both young and old which has the added potential of being lucratively worthwhile.

2

BEACHCOMBING

For many hundreds of years, the fascinating and rewarding art of beachcombing has existed. It was once only a privileged few who would receive the doctrines, bequeathed by fathers and forefathers, of the sea's secrets and treasures; secrets which in the past could be exploited to provide a means of existence. Those possessing this hereditary knowledge were virtually sworn to secrecy and would only pass the doctrines to their children or someone especially close, for these were the days when living on a desolate coast meant a hard struggle for mere survival. Food could be obtained from various types of seaweed strewn across the beach, or from rock pools where the sea had deposited crabs and other welcome creatures. The well-trained eye of the beachcomber could find amber and other valuable gems camouflaged among the pebbles, or sand-encrusted coins and trinkets lying on the shore. He would also know the complex and efficient distribution methods possessed by the sea and could determine the resting places of jewellery and other valuable items. The sites of shipwrecks would also be known to him, as well as the weather and sea conditions which might free some of the valuables the wreck held and distribute them to within his reach. Necessity developed this art to such an extent that it became almost a sixth sense for many beachcombers. The sea provided for all needs and in turn transformed the people into something like sea creatures themselves.

An old gentleman enlists the help of a metal detector while beachcombing.

Ten exceptionally valuable eighteenth-century Portuguese coins found on the beach at Ilfracombe, Devon, after a storm. The badly worn coin on the bottom right is a Spanish cob, an example of the treasure more commonly known as 'pieces of eight'.

Much of the old beachcombing knowledge and technique died when the practice changed from a trade to a hobby but today, with the astounding increase in interest and participants, the old skills are being rediscovered. Although the coastline and beaches have changed with time, the sea's habits remain the same and its treasures remain inexhaustible. Beachcombing today can and indeed does provide an entire means of existence, in the same manner that it did hundreds of years ago, and the modern beachcomber has the added advantages of equipment and facilities which modern technology has supplied. The history of our coasts can be discovered in literature instead of whispered by father to son as it was many years ago. A beachcomber today can also choose to employ modern equipment such as land or underwater metal detectors. But here we are concerned only with the traditional methods of beachcombing: learning to discover the treasures of the sea through observation, awareness and the essential knowledge of the sea's distribution methods.

Although the same basic principles of beachcombing apply on every beach, there is on every beach a lifetime of learning which may be developed, with practice, to a fine art until the beachcomber knows every inch of the beach and where the 'glory holes', as they are called, are to be found. Glory holes are the areas of beach where the sea persistently deposits valuables according to their weight, size and surface area. It may be a rock crevice where rings are left by the tide, or a patch of shingle where the sea deposits coins. Once these glory holes or productive areas have been established and expertise has increased, that beach will remain generous to the enlightened beachcomber for years on end.

RESEARCH

The first consideration for any prospective beachcomber is to ponder over the types of treasures the sea may have to offer and the areas where losses are made before endeavouring to determine their final destination points. Contemplation on this is best achieved while on the beach where seaside events can be observed and considered. The majority of coastal treasures today take the form of modern coinage and jewellery in astounding abundance. For the source of this, one must look towards the inevitable carelessness of the hundreds of thousands of people who descend on Britain's beaches each day at the mere mention of summer. Since 1871, when Bank Holidays were initiated, the seaside industry has boomed, and the six thousand miles of Britain's coastline have been frequented by people of all ages and walks of life. It would be impossible to even begin to conceive the worth of the millions of coins which must have been lost in this time, or the value of jewellery and other valuables lost to the sea, but for a glimpse,

Modern valuables found on the beach by Elizabeth Green and family.

Sheila and Bert Freeman's exciting discovery of twenty-three well preserved Gallo-Belgic staters.

one has only to consider personal recollections of losses made on beaches. Virtually everyone who has ventured on to a beach must have experienced the sight of a coin silently slipping into the sand, leaving no trace whatsoever of its existence.

The sea's treasure hunting stock is forever being replenished with jewellery, by the swimmers who hurriedly wrap wrist-watches, necklaces, bracelets and other pieces of jewellery for 'safe keeping' inside their clothes, which only too often fall prey to the relentless sand. There are also the swimmers who prefer to wear their rings and other jewellery while swimming, oblivious of the fact that the cold water will contract fingers and release rings, or that the current will niggle at the safety catch of a bracelet or necklace until the sea claims yet another possession.

It is said that the sea keeps its secrets, but this is not completely the way, for occasionally the sea gives a quick and tantalizing glimpse of the secrets it possesses, and this occurs in the event of storms. It is at this time that the older treasures may be retrieved, when the rough seas and strong currents break open the rotting timbers of unknown shipwrecks or long forgotten sea-chests, and release the valuables which are conveyed shoreward by the tide. The threshing waves work at the shore, wrenching away at the sand and pebbles to expose the older treasures beneath. In the event of such a storm, and as soon as conditions permit, the beachcomber must work without delay to recover the articles deposited before the tide returns to collect its secrets once again. Such is the extent of valuables which are carried on a stormy sea that coins can be seen to roll in with the waves. It is not uncommon to make discoveries, such as the recent occurrence on Portobello Beach near Edinburgh, when 363 coins and three gold rings were harvested at the end of a recent storm by one Scottish treasure hunter. On a Devonshire beach, at Ilfracombe, ten rare and extremely valuable gold coins were the recent result of stormy seas which worked on an ancient shipwreck. The discoverers of these coins began searching when prevailing weather conditions were apparent and a storm seemed imminent. The loose soft sand had been stripped from the shore and deposited above the high tide line to form a bank and it was here that these coins were discovered, worth hundreds of pounds each.

TIDES AND CURRENTS

The most favourable period for beachcombing is the end of September to the beginning of March, with mid-November usually proving most productive. The strong winter tides erode the beach to expose the older treasures and summertime losses; the light summer tides replenish the beach with objects but also cover them with a great deal of sand and pebbles. Spending the winter months in serious searching also has the advantage of solitude, when one can work free from inquisitive souls and prostrate sun-soaking bodies. The summer months are far better spent in observing the areas where treasures are most likely to be lost, such as popular swimming areas, changing areas, ice cream stalls, deck-chair sites and so on, and by walking along the high and low tide line, training the eye to recognize small treasures which the sea has deposited. On a summertime stroll such as this, it is important to note the precise location of the tide lines, for although they are consistent throughout the summer months, they change with the stronger seas of autumn and winter. The high tide line is noticeable by a build-up of shingle or sand and deposit of seaweed, shells and other articles and its position should be compared with a permanent landmark such as a groyne, to be remembered as a productive beachcombing area in winter months.

The movement of the sea is influenced by the moon, which makes tides so consistent that their times of movement can be predicted for years ahead, with a matter of only minutes in variation. For the water to flow from one tide line to the other, it takes six hours and thirteen minutes, and this occurs four times every day of every year. It is useful to remember that high tide occurs approximately fifty minutes later each day. The types of tides greatly influence the strength of currents in the sea and, in turn, determine the conditions of productivity for the beachcomber. They are therefore a habit of the sea which should be understood and remembered. Since time immemorial those whose existence was influenced by the rise and fall of the sea, associated it with and studied it by the phases of the moon whose gravitational force directly influences the movement and timing of the tides.

There are two significant types of tides, known as a 'spring tide' and a 'neap tide'. The spring tide occurs at the new moon and full moon and the neap tide occurs in the moon's first and last quarters. The spring tide, which in fact occurs two days after the sun and moon are in conjunction (new moon) and opposite (full moon), provides the two occasions in the month, approximately a fortnight apart, when the tides range to their extremes and the lowest low tide and the highest high tide occur. At the time of the spring tide, currents are stronger than at the neap tide, thus distributing more and heavier matter from the sea bed which is deposited on the shore. The neap tide, which occurs two days after the sun and moon are in quadrature (first and last quarters), produces the smallest range of tide, when low water is at its highest and high water is at its lowest. Neap tides alternate with spring tides, their currents are weak and they convey less matter to the shore.

One more tide which is of great significance to the beachcomber is that of the equinoctial spring tide which occurs only twice a year, around 21 March and 23 September. These spring tides are the greatest of all and good beachcombing conditions are to be expected.

THE WIND
The force of the wind is also a major contributing factor to beachcombing conditions, for the harder the wind blows, the

stronger the currents become. When the prevailing wind has been blowing in the same direction for two days or more, the beach will be replenished with greater treasures. Recognizing the direction of the wind is an art which will quickly be developed during the summertime strolls along the beach as one's awareness and observation increase. Assistance in developing this awareness is given by noticing the direction in which the tops of the waves break and the direction in which boats turn on their moorings.

DISTRIBUTION

It has been established then, that tides, currents and wind affect the quality and quantity of a beachcomber's finds and from this a knowledge is gained of when to search beaches. To obtain the knowledge of where to search beaches, a close investigation must be made of the distribution methods possessed by the sea. This again, is an understanding which is developed by observing the characteristics of the sea and shore and, in each particular case, the layout of the shore.

Even the most casual glance at a beach, especially if it is of pebbles, will reveal to the observer that the sea acts as a vast and extremely efficient sorting office, displaying the material it has deposited as though it has been filed according to its size. The sea files its goods according to their weight, size and surface area, depositing heavy material at the high tide line and working down progressively to the low tide line. It is for this reason that glory holes occur when the sea files coins, rings or other valuables in their respective positions. Although the points of these glory holes should be marked and remembered upon discovery, one should also bear in mind that their positions will change according to the force of currents and tides.

From this information, one could deduce that coins must be found in the areas of beach which display pebbles of the equivalent weight and shape as a coin. This would be a reasonable assumption and provides a general guide to follow, but when the surface area of a different object, such as a ring, is taken into account, the rule cannot be applied so easily. A ring possesses so little surface area to be propelled by the sea that it would be carried at the same rate, and deposited in the same areas, as much heavier objects.

This, however, is not all which determines the resting places of the sea's treasures, for this information only determines the object's position *up* the beach from the shore. To determine its travel *along* the beach, one must take into account the subject of 'long shore drift'. This, quite simply, is the direction in which material is carried along the beach, the effects of which may be easily noticed. Groynes are erected on many beaches to check this movement and prevent too much material moving towards one end of the beach. The direction of long shore drift is dependent upon the prevailing wind and is easily recognized by noting on which side of the groynes, or other obstacles, shingle or sand build-up occurs. When the direction of this drift has been determined, the beachcomber then knows the direction that treasures will take from the sites of wrecks, popular swimming areas, piers and so on.

Considerable research has been undertaken in the USA, and some in Britain, to determine the behaviour of material which the sea carries, endeavouring to discover an object's movement on and off the shore and its travel along the beach. The motive for such research is to protect the shoreline and discover more efficient techniques of checking long shore drift than groynes which, although fairly effective, necessitate the frequent use of bulldozers on the beach to remove the build-up of sand and shingle. The beachcomber can greatly benefit from this research and should keep in contact with any new procedures developing from it. Various beachcombers have also undertaken their own studies by planting a number of marked objects on the beach and checking their position and progress before they are claimed by the sea, and then endeavouring to discover their point of destination.

The behaviour of material carried by the sea does, of course, differ from one beach to another, but the general and popular conclusions reached by all interested parties have been as follows. An item which is manually deposited between the high and low tide line of a beach, for instance a coin, is virtually covered by sand or shingle after two flood (incoming) tides. Throughout average weather conditions the coin experiences no movement, but immediately high wind conditions develop, or at the first spring tide it experiences, the coin is removed by harsher waves and stronger currents and commences its travel. A breaking wave has a 'swash' and a 'backwash'. The swash moves the coin up the beach and the backwash drags it back towards the sea. The swash loses its momentum as it climbs further up the slope of the beach while the backwash increases its influence as it returns down towards the sea. For this reason the coin, which is a light object, is moved back and forth within the low tide line quarter of the beach. This swash and backwash procedure is, however, affected by the prevailing wind, unless the wind blows directly on shore. As is more often the case, the prevailing wind blows at an angle to the shore and the backwash will be affected, dragging its coin in the direction of the wind. The coin now moves progressively along the shore in the direction of long shore drift, remaining still for a few days when currents are weak. The movement pattern is interrupted in the event of high wave activity and especially if stormy seas occur, when the coin moves higher up the beach towards the high tide line. As the seas settle, the coin too settles in this new position. When the backwash has insufficient strength to transport the coin further, it gradually becomes concealed by heavier items and tends to sink lower and lower, where it remains until activated again by a violent storm. On a sandy beach, the coin will sink to a depth where it reaches the 'hardpack' sand which is the hard layer on which the upper soft sand rests.

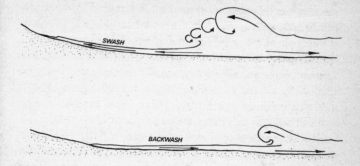

The directional pulls on a breaking wave.

This is only a general observation, for results will vary according to the characteristics of each beach. A fascinating and rewarding project may be carried out by the beachcomber to assist him in a better understanding of his sea and shore, using simple items such as coin-shaped metal discs.

OUTLAY AND EQUIPMENT

One of the most wonderful aspects of beachcombing as a form of treasure hunting is that it requires no financial outlay or real hard work. It offers a distinct increase in one's mental and physical health, and develops one's awareness drastically. The beachcomber's eyes will soon adopt a new and accurate faculty, whereby treasures camouflaged on the beach will be immediately spotted. It may be likened to spotting fish which swim camouflaged in the sea: once one has been spotted, many more will become apparent.

For the beginner, it is advisable to discover the effects of the sea on various metals: copper, for instance, is turned green and silver is turned black. Except for gold, which is an inert metal and unaltered by the elements, the sea has an uncanny knack of painting its own colours on the treasures it has claimed, as though in an attempt to brand them all as its undisputed possessions. Such brands, however, may be removed by the beach-comber, as will be shown in Chapter 14.

There is no piece of equipment which is essential to the beachcomber, though one very useful implement is a large garden-type sieve, or a plastic grocer's scoop which may be adapted by cutting away its back section and replacing it with thin wire mesh, or a chip-frying basket. This can save a great deal of time and can also increase the number of finds.

Beachcombing with a metal detector is a relatively recent innovation and one cannot deny that this is an extremely efficient way of discovering the sea's treasures. It *is* possible to stumble upon finds with no knowledge of the sea's secrets whatsoever, though treasures will be found few and far between, for one cannot expect to point the instrument blindly to wind, follow one's nose and expect success. A happy medium may be discovered whereby the detector is used as well as one's eyes and the essential knowledge of the sea's distribution methods. For the beachcomber and metal detector user, it is important that one commences the hobby as a beach-comber and only introduces the metal detector when experience, knowledge and awareness have been established.

3
METAL DETECTING

It would be a difficult task to find any person who, at the mere mention of metal detecting, does not show enthusiasm or have a desire to at least try the hobby, for rarely a week now passes without a press report of some valuable discovery being made by a metal detecting enthusiast. This continual publicity has greatly contributed to removing the public's naïvity of the hobby. It was, after all, only a few years ago that the popular belief was that these instruments were mine detectors left over from the Second World War and the operator, if seen using one on a beach, was a figure to be left well alone. But such is the growth of the hobby, that over 80,000 people are now metal detector users in Britain and an estimated 3,000 more join this figure every month.

MOTIVES

So what does entice so many people to become involved in treasure hunting with a metal detector? Many are inspired by the increasing number of valuable coin hoards which continue to be discovered all over the country and are therefore attracted by the 'get rich quick' proposition. This of course appeals to us all, but in the case of metal detecting, great disillusion is usually the result. There are others who are attracted by the mere concept of treasure hunting, and those two romantic words certainly suggest fulfilment of desires common to all, of discovering rustic sea-chests festooned with gold and exotic jewels. Again a disappointment is in store, for this attractive concept is far removed from the reality which awaits a modern day treasure hunter.

The motives for embarking upon the hobby should be to find an interesting and rewarding pastime which combines luck with skill, creates a fascinating, knowledgeable and healthy outlook, plus the bonus of being a lucrative sideline. Those who commence the hobby with expectations such as these cannot fail to find an absorbing and successful pastime. Of the three thousand new detectors which are sold each month, there are probably only a few hundred which are used to their full potential and not left to accumulate dust in a cupboard. The majority of novice treasure hunters are so overwhelmed with apprehension and high expectations that no forethought or research is undertaken and within a month or so of darting around the countryside with this new-found hobby enthusiasm is exhausted, detectors are pronounced useless and soon appear in the 'For Sale' column of the local paper.

RESEARCH
It must be realized that a metal detector constitutes only half of the hobby and of success, for it is the operator who must decide where and how to apply it. Without understanding how his metal detector works and how artefacts are lost, the operator's efforts are futile, as in the case of the beachcomber who starts at one end of the beach searching every inch of sand in front of him. Treasures are not evenly distributed beneath the ground but greatly concentrated in certain areas, the location of which can only be discovered through careful observations and research. The amateur treasure hunter fast evolves into a budding historian, spending many hours poring over books to lead him on his never-ending treasure trail.

Philip Connolly of Gravesend, Kent, completed two years of

careful research before he discovered a hoard of beautiful gold nobles worth £8,000. Although his research had been long and painstaking, he was well rewarded by the discovery. It took him a mere twenty minutes to recover the majority of the hoard of seven Edward III and Richard II nobles and half-nobles. The other four nobles were discovered on subsequent trips. Philip detects regularly, using his knowledge of history and observation, and his finds are typical of what an enthusiastic treasure hunter may recover. He has discovered about two thousand coins, mainly dating from Victorian days, excluding modern currency. His jewellery collection consists of more than a dozen gold and silver rings, a dozen or so bracelets and necklaces, and his extensive collection of miscellaneous artefacts includes horse brasses, medieval cow and sheep bells, buttons, tokens, lighters, musket balls and so on. His hobby rarely takes him further than his immediate area. He merely takes full advantage of local history to assist him and uses the full potential and understanding he has for his detector.

BUYING A DETECTOR

The first consideration for the prospective metal detector user is that of choosing and purchasing a suitable machine, which for the complete novice can too often be a bewildering task. It would be easy to fall prey to the trap of buying a relatively inexpensive make or model, only to discover in a few months' time that one's capabilities had surpassed such an inferior machine. Similarly, it would be equally as frustrating to purchase one of the most expensive machines, only to discover shortly afterwards that the enthusiasm of the hobby had dwindled and expectations been thwarted. However, there is usually a happy medium between the two extremes; one can compromise by buying a good quality detector, which is not too advanced in its operation or so highly priced that an expensive disappointment could be in store. Prices of metal

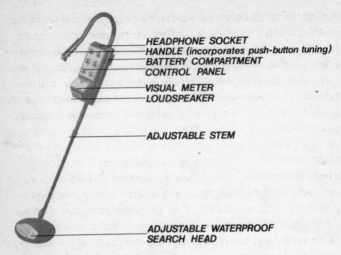

HEADPHONE SOCKET
HANDLE (incorporates push-button tuning)
BATTERY COMPARTMENT
CONTROL PANEL
VISUAL METER
LOUDSPEAKER

ADJUSTABLE STEM

ADJUSTABLE WATERPROOF
SEARCH HEAD

The basic parts of a metal detector.

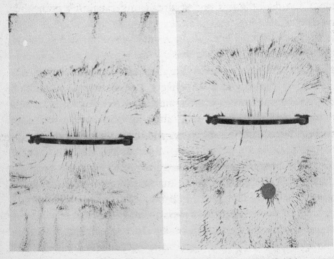

The search coil of a metal detector produces an electro-magnetic field.

The electro-magnetic field is disturbed by the presence of a coin.

detectors fluctuate a great deal but for some time in the past and within the foreseeable future, £60 is the approximate financial outlay which must be considered. There are, however, many different makes and models on the market with as many technical terms to confuse the customer, so a basic knowledge of how a metal detector works and what expectations one should have of it is therefore essential before purchase.

HOW A METAL DETECTOR WORKS

Metal detectors contain a wire coil and when an electrical current is passed through this coil, an electro-magnetic field is produced. If a metal object is placed within the electro-magnetic field, it creates a disturbance which changes the electrical current passing through the search coil. This change is measured and emitted as a signal by the metal detector. This, very basically, is how a metal detector works but a little more should be explained regarding its capabilities for the interest of the prospective buyer.

'Ground effect' is a term which will no doubt be used many times by the salesman who may often over-emphasize this problem, endeavouring to sell higher-priced models which are capable of eliminating these effects. It was mentioned earlier that a metal detector's electro-magnetic field is disturbed by the presence of a metal object, but to be more precise, it is the presence of any object which conducts electricity. When this object is placed within range of the detector's electro-magnetic field, it is transformed into a temporary electro-magnet, and is thus detected. This conductive matter not only includes metal objects but also seawater and rainwater, one of which is unfortunately present in most soils and disturbs the electro-magnetic field produced by the detector. This phenomenon is known as 'ground effect'. The earth itself contains conductive properties which contribute greatly towards ground effect. Compared to the signal which will be produced by a coin, the

Measuring the depth penetration of a new metal detector with an old penny.

The correct way to hold a metal detector.

A selection of Edward I and Edward II half-nobles and Richard II quarter-nobles picked up with a metal detector.

reaction produced by ground effect is gradual and the metal detector operator soon becomes accustomed to differentiating between the two. There are, however, detectors which have a ground exclusion facility which, although in no way essential, is an undisputed advantage if one wishes to detect in a heavily mineralized or wet sand soil and can seriously affect the performance of an ordinary detector.

Discriminator detectors are also available, which again are in a higher price bracket. In the hands of the experienced detector user they can save a great deal of time and effort. The discriminator enables one to avoid digging up tin cans, silver paper, bottle tops, rusty nails, ring pull tabs from drink cans and other undesirable objects, which can be a frustrating aspect of metal detecting. When working a site such as a popular beauty spot, fairground or picnic area, there is a predominance of these articles, though at the same time there will undoubtedly be valuables.

Discriminators, unlike conventional detectors, do not measure the total change in the signal, they measure the change at a precise point in the signal's wave form. This method of choosing a 'sampling point' enables certain items to be ignored or to produce the reverse signal to that obtained by a conventional 'all metal' detector. The position of this sampling point determines which metals are discriminated against. All metals above the sampling point give the normal positive signal, all metals below give a negative signal (see diagram).

Ground effect can also be eliminated by choosing the appropriate sampling point. However, it is not possible to eliminate ground effect and discriminate at the same time because the sampling points occur in different positions. Recently, metal detector manufacturers have produced detectors which have two modes of operation, ground exclusion and discrimination, enabling the operator to search in the ground exclusion mode and switch to the discrimination mode to identify the find.

It is of paramount importance when buying a detector to test its performance in the stockist's showroom, before making any decisions. The ideal detector should be light but robust, well balanced, comfortable to hold, adjustable in length and simple to operate. It should have a water-immersible search head, and adequate depth penetration.

One of the questions most frequently asked by those interested in metal detectors is, 'How deep will it detect?' This is a matter which depends greatly upon the size of the object and, to a lesser degree, on the type of soil. It also varies from one detector type to another. This can be tested in the showroom by laying the detector horizontally on a table with the search head protruding over the edge and adjusted at right angles to the detector's stem. With the use of an object such as an old

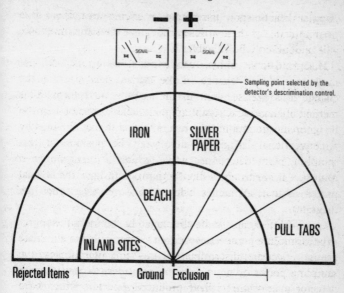

Diagram illustrating the scale of conductivity of items which can be discriminated against with metal detectors. The conductivity on one item does not necessarily start where the previous one finishes.

English penny, the detector's depth penetration will be discovered. It should be remembered, however, that the detection depth, generally speaking, will be greater in air than in the ground because the object is not masked by ground effect. A detector with a detection range of approximately ten inches on an old English penny is normally satisfactory.

Upon purchase of a detector, a brief guide may be given by the salesman on the methods of use and operating instructions usually accompany the unit. This is, however, definitely no passport to competence. Very rarely does one receive absolute beginner's luck with no knowledge of the hobby's techniques, though it cannot be denied that this has occasionally occurred. For example, there is the recent case of Mr Peter O'Nion of

Rotherham, South Yorkshire, who, after spending no more than four hours in trying out his metal detector, received a slight signal which he thought was no more than ground effect. He decided to investigate it to help himself to understand the difference between ground effect and the presence of metal. While standing over the signal, his brother assisted him in tuning the metal detector properly and Peter commenced digging. At a depth of four inches the signal became stronger and Peter's enthusiasm increased when he noticed a silver and green coin in the hole he had dug, which he guessed to be an old sixpence or threepence. The signal still increased and at a depth of fourteen inches a layer of stones were found and beneath it an earthenware pot containing 3,501 copper and silver dipped Roman coins. Fortunately, he was advised by a friend to take the pot, weighing two and a half stone, immediately to the local museum. An inquest followed to decide whether or not the hoard was treasure trove; when a discovery is declared treasure trove, the finder receives the full market value from the museums, should they wish to retain it for historical interest – and this was the case with Peter's find.

An example such as this is an exception and only goes to prove the vast amount of such treasures which await the treasure hunter who is experienced in using a detector and has completed some research. Hoards such as this, and many other valuables and curios, are continually coming to light. In times of war and unrest, a great many people chose to secrete their valuables in the soil; banks and safes were not in existence and any form of wealth meant a dangerous life. But before so much as considering a hunt for such hoards, one should familiarize oneself with the detector, for persistent success is only achieved when the operator leads the metal detector and not vice versa. There is a great deal of skill in using a metal detector and the key is complete understanding of the machine, which can be developed to such a degree that it becomes almost an extension of the arm. It is by no means uncommon for treasure hunters to acquire a kind of sixth sense when they have gained a certain amount of understanding and experience in the hobby. There have been many cases where an experienced treasure hunter has on occasion ignored research, observation and systematic searching and relied purely on intuition, often with astoundingly successful results.

HOW TO USE A METAL DETECTOR

Once a satisfactory detector has been chosen, it should be persevered with until its performance is mastered. There is no better site on which to commence these preliminaries than in one's own garden. The assistance and company of an experienced operator is a great aid, but for the many who cannot achieve this, a guide dedicated to the novice is given here.

Commence by adjusting the detector to a comfortable length so that the search head rests no more than an inch above the ground. It is important that the detector is tuned whilst in this position and that the distance between the ground and the search head is maintained throughout the search. If at any point the distance exceeds an inch, then the search head will be too high and depth penetration will be lost.

Methods of tuning vary greatly from one detector to another. The best method to follow is that of the operator instructions which accompany the machine upon purchase, and then experiment to find the point of tuning at which maximum efficiency is obtained. This will be discovered by burying a coin two or three inches beneath the soil and playing around with the control knobs to find where the best signal is produced.

This method will greatly help in understanding the detector's performance but to memorize the position of the controls is not a total solution, for the tuning varies drastically according to the type of soil, the temperature of the ground, sloping or uneven ground, presence of water and, to a lesser degree, condition of batteries. It is advisable to tune the detector to emit a continual faint tone, for this will act as a constant reminder that the detector is still in tune and enables the operator to distinguish more easily the signal produced by ground effect and the signal produced by an object. Nothing can be more frustrating than to discover that time has been wasted by being unaware that the detector had gone out of tune. By tuning the detector to emit a faint tone, the ground effect can also be measured and checked accordingly throughout the search.

It is merely a case of trial and error before the characteristics of ground effect are understood. Every novice treasure hunter experiences the frustration of chasing elusive and phantom signals before being able to look back in wonder at the bewilderment it once caused. As a very general guide, it will be noticed that the signal from ground effect is a gradual change in tone as opposed to the abrupt 'blip' produced by a coin or similar object. It should be mentioned however, that some sites are virtually unusable due to the amount of ground effect; other sites seem devoid of the problem. If particular difficulty is experienced on the chosen site, use a different location before condemning the detector as faulty and returning to its vendor.

When the tuning has been mastered, various items may be buried which will serve as excellent training in understanding the types of sounds to listen for. A coin resting on its side (which is quite common, especially on ploughed land and beaches) may easily be ignored unless the operator is aware of the slight sound it will produce. The use of headphones, which often accompany a detector upon purchase, is an undisputed advantage. They effectively increase the depth penetration which may be obtained from the detector by enabling the faintest signals to be heard. They also obliterate external noises such as traffic or the sound of waves on the seashore. The detector's search head should be swept fairly slowly back and forth, moving forward and overlapping the last sweep by

An experienced treasure hunter, Philip Connolly has dug up over two thousand coins of historic value quite apart from a great collection of miscellaneous items such as hinges, buttons and utensils.

The collection shown in this photograph is the result of only two months' searching.

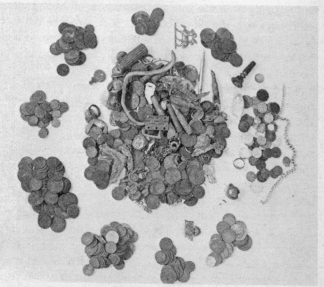

Peter O'Nion and his son testing metal detectors in their garden.

The line and pins method ensures a very thorough coverage of the area.

Extracting a find with care so the turf may be replaced easily.

approximately two inches to ensure all the ground is covered by the pick-up area. A common mistake made by many beginners is to raise the detector too high from the ground at either end of the sweep, or as it would be in this case, the 'swing'. A slow and methodical search of a site is advantageous, for not only are there more results achieved by this method, but the operator also knows that the area has been thoroughly searched.

A method which is used by many metal detector users, especially if a productive site has been discovered, is the 'line and pins' technique. This is achieved by dividing up the area with string attached to a pin at each end, thus enabling a thorough search of each strip of ground to be made. A method such as this would be used on an area such as an ancient fairground, where many valuable discoveries are to be made, and when the treasure hunter needs to feel assured that he has recovered everything from the site before moving on. The line

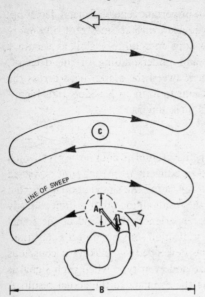

The sweep method of searching. A: the width of the detector's pick-up area. B: the length of a comfortable sweep. C: A concealed metal object.

and pins technique is invariably used when a scattered hoard has been discovered. A scattering of coins is quite common, especially on farmland where the action of a plough may have broken a pot which formerly contained the hoard, and scattered the contents around the area. Burrowing animals are also an agent of this.

It will be noticed that the ground is inexhaustible of treasures, for not only is it being continually replenished with modern valuables but the earth also has a percolating effect upon objects in the soil. Any gardener will be aware of the manner in which flints continue to work their way to the surface and, as with treasures, the process is expedited in the event of heavy rain. Once a good site is found, it should not be forgotten after it has been thoroughly searched, as it may yield many more objects later. This phenomenon appears to occur to a greater extent on hilltop sites.

Pinpointing a find is an important aspect of metal detecting, for it makes recovery quicker, neater and generally more efficient. This soon develops into quite a skill as accuracy increases with practice and understanding of the detector. When a signal is obtained, sweep the search head across the area from opposite directions to form an X shape, thus identifying where the signal is most intense.

RETRIEVING FINDS

Extracting the find from the ground is another aspect which should be developed into an efficient art. Much time is wasted through sifting earth and relocating the signal and, apart from being a tedious process, the result all too often is unnecessarily large holes. With a little experience, the sound of the signal will provide an exact indication of the object's position. Expertise in this may be developed by making a conscious estimate of the find's size and even type when each signal is obtained, and comparing the estimate to the actual result. A competent metal detector user can predetermine an object's approximate length and width, and often its type, (i.e. a nail, coin, etc.).

Tidiness must be regarded as the most important consideration in retrieving finds, for the hobby of metal detecting is in constant danger of being banned due to a few thoughtless people who neglect to fill in their holes after extracting finds. Apart from the unattractiveness of such a display, the dangers to the public are limitless. It cannot be overstressed that every hole, no matter how small, should be filled and each site used should be left exactly as it was found, if the hobby is to have its reputation repaired and its existence permitted.

Various implements may be used to extract a find, the largest of which should be a small garden trowel. The use of a shovel is not only unnecessary but it is likely to result in refused permission by any landowner. A penknife, a screwdriver, a bricklayer's fine-pointed trowel; any small implement is suitable and the technique is simply to cut three sides in the turf, flap this back, extract the find, replace any loose earth and the flap of turf, treading it firm again. It is often inevitable that on well-cared-for turf, such as a garden lawn, traces of earth will remain for a few days or until the event of rain, and it will be quite apparent that some kind of digging activity has taken place. When using a site such as a garden lawn or recreation ground, where it is imperative that the site is left clean, or if one wishes to impress a formerly dubious landowner, the problem may be solved simply by using a small square of plastic sheeting and placing any earth extracted on this before pouring it back into the hole.

It should be mentioned here that archaeological sites are strictly taboo to the metaldetector user and it is illegal and punishable by a fine and/or imprisonment to plunder such sites. It is imperative that permission is sought before detecting on any private property, for it is otherwise classed as trespass and the removal of finds as stealing. The legal aspects of metal detecting are dealt with in detail in Chapter 15, but these points should be remembered no matter where one chooses to search.

4
DUMP DIGGING

Yesterday's throwaways are often today's treasures and there is no better site on which to discover this than on the ancient dumping grounds. During the last ten years, Britain has 'taken to the bottle' in a big way. For in an age dedicated to planned obsolescence and unattractive plastic throwaway containers, nostalgia hunters up and down the country delve into the old Edwardian, Victorian and often earlier dumping grounds, on a quest for the artistic charm and valuable discoveries which await them. Not only does the hobby provide attractive collections and an enthralling and educational pastime but a good living may be made when opportunities are exploited. Bottles are amongst the most common finds and some rare specimens will fetch £200 or more at auctions. The attractive painted pot lids, which in Victorian times were designed to be discarded after the contents were consumed, fetch anything up to £500 each.

The types of discoveries which may be made on these dumps are endless, the majority of which are now valuable collectors items. Amongst the many other items which a dump digger will discover are clay pipes, porcelain dolls, pots and jars which once contained cosmetics, foodstuffs, alcoholic beverages, drugs, miracle cures and poisons. Attractive ornaments may be found such as vases, figurines, boxes and many small trinkets. Antique household equipment such as

Dump digging on a typical site.

flat-irons, ink bottles, bed-warming and feet-warming bottles, cutlery, baby feeders and so on, all await discovery. Fortunately, all these articles are of a highly durable nature, even those intended for disposal, and a great deal still lie intact today.

BACKGROUND

Today it is accepted that refuse disposal is undertaken by the council once a week and one can imagine the dilemma which would result should this facility be relinquished. But it was not long ago that coping with your own household rubbish was an accepted part of life. Every house or housing community had what was known as a 'muck hole', and all unwanted matter would be put there. When the area was full and in need of removal, it would be taken to the communal village or town dump. At one time it was collected by persons who would sort through the contents to find saleable items and thus earn their

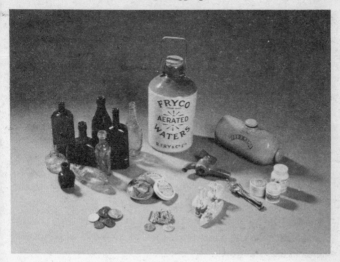

Household articles of varying dates likely to be found in a dump.

living, or by brick-making factories who would extract and use the ashes to make bricks and dump the remainder nearby. This practice was gradually discontinued as the disposal of more and more rubbish became necessary. The most widely used method, therefore, was for the man of the house to borrow a horse and cart from the local farmer and transport the rubbish to the local tip.

In towns in later years, when sites large enough for rubbish were used up, refuse was transported out into the country by rail, barge or horse and cart. The refuse of London, for instance, was regularly transported to the south-east of England.

It is difficult, for the inexperienced, to imagine the vast amount of treasures which may be found on a dump, but literally anything is possible and awaiting recovery. In the days when there was little in the way of transport, moving house or spring cleaning would result in many articles being discarded;

articles which were then virtually worthless, but today could command a fortune. There are also the treasures found on dumps which, regardless of time, could never be fitted into the category of rubbish: treasures such as coins, watches, jewellery, etc. which evolve from accidental losses. One only has to consider personal losses to gain a glimpse of the treasures which lie amongst the rubbish tips. At least once a year, everyone must experience the frustration of a lost item around the home which, despite extensive searches, fails to be recovered, leaving only the explanation that it must have disappeared with the rubbish. For instance, the lighter which fell unnoticed from the writing desk to the waste-paper bin, or the article of jewellery which was 'posted' to the dustbin by the young child. Consider the number of people who would use a local dump site and a fair estimation of its worth in accidental losses alone, should be achieved.

LOCATING DUMPS

Discovering the location of a dump should never present a problem once some knowledge has been gained of recognition of likely sites. Many are of course obliterated beneath housing developments and the major city dumps are likely to be well worked by other dump digging enthusiasts, but many hundreds of equally productive smaller dumps are to be discovered almost anywhere.

A couple who recently moved to a house in Dunbartonshire discovered that their garden was resting on top of the old village dump and it produced for them many beautiful and valuable items. A private dump such as this is sometimes found, for when village dumps were filled to the maximum, a layer of earth was put over them to level the area, over which buildings were sometimes erected. When hunting for the site of a dump one never has to travel far, for on the outskirts of every town or village there would have been at least one such site. The Victorians usually chose their sites carefully and

certain areas in the landscape are more likely to conceal a
·dumping ground than others. These locations are explained in
detail in Chapters 8–12 concerning treasure hunting sites, as
too are the methods of recognizing dump sites by the natural
vegetation they encourage.

RECOVERING ITEMS FROM A DUMP

The techniques of dump digging are also important, for an
efficient but cautious method must be followed. Once a productive dump has been established (and permission obtained
to search it), a methodical approach should be used in order to
receive maximum results. On the majority of dumps it will be
found that the productivity occurs in layers: the topsoil which
covers the matter is unproductive, progressing through layers
which donate results according to the year, and then occasionally a dividing layer of soil which underneath reveals another
dump of an earlier period. Clearly then one should be
prepared for some fairly extensive digging. The most common
mistake made by many beginners is to dig many small holes
here and there, instead of choosing an area of the dump and
digging a trench in it. A minimum depth of three feet for a
trench is usually necessary and the width should be one in
which a shovel may be used comfortably. When satisfied that
all has been recovered from that area, one may then move forward, using the extracted earth to fill in the trench behind. By
building up this bank behind oneself, the risk of the trench
collapsing is eliminated and the task of lifting heavy shovels of
earth above the head is avoided. After each session of digging,
the earth should be raked level again. This final tidying-up
process is also advantageous in that it usually reveals the odd
clay pipe or small trinket which has inevitably been missed.

EQUIPMENT

The individual will soon discover which tool he prefers to use;
it will soon be realized that the conventional garden shovel,

Down in the dumps, Kate Johnson discovers a horse shoe for good luck and a Victorian medicine bottle after only a few minutes' digging.

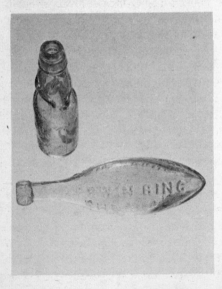

The Codd bottle (*above*) and the Hamilton bottle are perhaps the most interesting examples of glassware to be found in a dump.

fork, and rake are generally unsuitable. Conventional shovels, in particular those with curved sides, prove destructive and require considerable effort to use. A flat spade, preferably pointed, is the most popular. A fork is always needed in addition as it is a far less destructive implement when a layer of valuables has been reached, and the smaller this fork is, the better. A small garden trowel may be used successfully to ease out objects packed into the earth. The modern garden rake invariably proves too shallow for tidying a site and results in a laborious task. A good old fashioned hoe is suitable though difficult to acquire, but as with most hobbies, the art of improvisation comes into its own, and the dump digger usually gets the tool he requires by constructing it himself.

Little equipment is necessary when dump digging, but there are some items which are invaluable. A pair of hard wearing industrial gloves, or at least a pair of rubber gloves, will help to avoid being cut by broken glass and decrease the risk of infection. It may at first appear to be distasteful to sift through rubbish and expose oneself to a wide selection of germs, but in fact the risk of infection is surprisingly low, provided preventative measures are taken. It is advocated that dump diggers should take the precaution of inoculation against tetanus, and that any cuts or grazes are sufficiently protected. It will be discovered that unpleasant odours do not exist on an old dump either and the reason for this is that the plant life around uses all rotting matter in the earth as an essential part of its growth, thereby cleansing the dump.

The only other equipment which is necessary on site is some cardboard boxes with a few rags in which to wrap the more delicate articles. Just what one wishes to discard and what to keep is purely a matter of taste, though for the beginner it is often a difficult decision. The usual and perhaps the best solution is to keep all the finds until they can be taken home, cleaned and identified. One should never make the mistake of throwing away an item which is of value but broken or in-

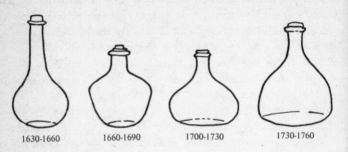

| 1630-1660 | 1660-1690 | 1700-1730 | 1730-1760 |

Approximate dates of different shapes of bottle.

complete. The discovery of half a clay pipe for instance is not uncommon, but neither is it uncommon for the other half to turn up close by. When, in former times, an item was broken, the pieces would be thrown on the rubbish tip together and would not stray far apart on reaching the dump site. Pot lids which have received rough treatment in transportation to the dump may be collected and restored.

IDENTIFYING FINDS

Archaeologists and ecologists have for many years been using dumps to understand better the ways of life and economy of our ancestors, but apart from the historical interest in the people who used the articles, much more learning and fascination awaits the dump digger in discovering the origins of the actual items.

Glassware is usually predominant on these grounds, usually in the form of bottles from the Victorian period and before. Bottle making began about 1000 BC mainly to hold ointments. These early containers were crudely made from sand, but by the first century BC the method of glass blowing commenced. The Syrians were the first to use moulds made of wood or clay and from these supplied the Romans with containers for

1760-1780   1770-1820   1820-1880   1840-1930

liquids. In the mid-sixteenth century, sealed bottles were being used in Britain to contain wine. These bottles, decorated with a seal, were blown without the use of moulds and resulted in a wide variety of interesting shapes and sizes. The bottles belonged to the gentry and nobility who would mark them with a seal for identification and send them to the wine merchants. Sealed bottles today command a high price from dealers and, although rare, have been known to turn up on dump sites.

Iron moulds were used in the early eighteenth century, and bottle making became widespread over Britain. Great ingenuity was shown in the design of early bottles; for instance, the Hamilton bottles of the early 1800s were shaped round at the bottom to prevent them being stood upright which would cause the cork to dry and shrink, allowing air to enter and the fizz to escape. Another famous design, called the Codd bottle, was patented by Hiram Codd in 1878. The struggle to keep the fizz in the bottle was still continuing and the earlier Hamilton bottle proved difficult to store. The Codd bottle was given two pinches in the neck which trapped a round glass stopper inside the bottle. By gas pressure, this stopper was forced against a rubber ring at the top of the bottle but it could

| 1630 - 1660 | 1660 - 1680 | 1680 - 1740 | 1700 - 1740 |

| 1740 - 1750 | 1750 - 1800 | 1800 - 1820 | 1820 - 1850 | 1850 - 1920 |

Approximate dates of different shapes of bottle necks.

be pushed down by a cap and plunger (provided with the bottle) to allow the contents to be poured. This crimp-necked bottle system was used until the 1920s when the screw stopper was introduced and most bottles were made by automatic machines.

DATING FINDS

To gain a better understanding of the hobby and the history of the dump on which one works, it is important to be able to date finds. Recognizing the period of finds is also essential when considering the value of discoveries. It is a relatively easy task to date bottles, firstly because it is a well documented subject and secondly because there are many indications in the shape and markings of a bottle. The shape of a bottle's body gives a rough guide as to the period in which it was made and the appearance of the bottle's neck also denotes the age. Many bottles have marks, numbers or writing on them, which enables a more accurate opinion to be given. Set out overleaf are some guide lines one should consider when dating a bottle by its markings.

Diamond-shaped registration marks came into being in 1842.

The names of manufacturing companies which are 'Limited' were formed after 1855.

The mention of 'trade mark' brings the date up to 1862 and after.

'Rd. No.' written on the bottle signifies it to be after 1884.

The word 'England' dates it from 1891.

Registration numbers began on 1 January 1884 and ran as follows with each serial number commencing on 1 January.

Registration No.	Year of Registration
1	1884
19754	1885
40480	1886
64520	1887
90483	1888
116648	1889
141273	1890
163767	1891
185713	1892
205240	1893
224720	1894
246975	1895
268392	1896
291241	1897
311658	1898
331707	1899
351202	1900
368154	1901
385088	1902
402913	1903
425017	1904
447548	1905
471486	1906
492487	1907
518415	1908
534963	1909

Pottery abounds on every dump site, most of which appears in fragments on the surface, but beneath the soil many complete articles will be discovered. When considering the age of pottery, one should not be deluded by the date (if any) which is

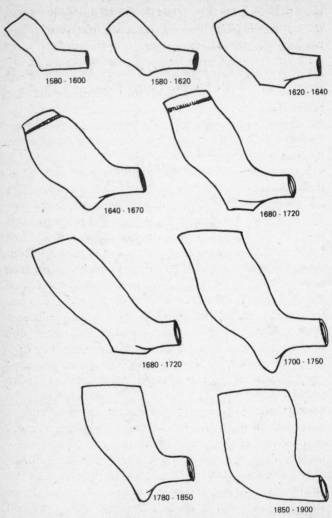

1580 - 1600

1580 - 1620

1620 - 1640

1640 - 1670

1680 - 1720

1680 - 1720

1700 - 1750

1780 - 1850

1850 - 1900

The shape of the bowl of a clay pipe gives the probable date of its manufacture.

written on the piece. Very rarely does this date signify the year of its making. Usually it is the date when the type of pottery was founded, which could lead to a disappointment. It is the pottery which offers no written details that suggests antiquity. On trade containers the absence of words such as 'Ltd', 'Trade Mark' or 'Reg. No.' usually means that the piece dates from before 1862.

Amongst the most sought-after pieces of pottery are Victorian underglaze printed pot lids which make an interesting and valuable collector's piece. The black-and-white variety command prices from £2 to £100 or more each, whilst those of coloured design can fetch prices up to or over £500. The prices depend, of course, upon condition, rarity and type. The pots formerly contained fish or meat pastes, drugs, toothpaste, or cosmetics and the black-and-white variety, which began in 1840, were intended for disposal after the contents were consumed. The coloured variety which date from 1860 were intended to be kept at the time of manufacture; it is therefore rare, but not unheard of, for these to be recovered from dumps. Pot lids display Victorian advertising at its best, in the form of beautiful designs and written details of the pot's contents, uses and often the name and address of the manufacturer or distributor. Magazines and books on the subject of pot lid collecting provide accurate dating material for the majority of pot lid types. For a rough guide, however, the general design and extent of workmanship on the lid offer an indication. Prints in blue ink and designs describing ointment to stimulate growth of the hair are typical of the earliest pot lids and date from around 1800, whilst the more common black-and-white variety were in use from 1840–1920. Pot lids which include pictures in addition to the painted borders began around 1885 and then in the late 1880s to the 1900s, pot lids of varying shapes appeared.

Collections of clay pipes can make a fascinating and varied display. They are the oldest of the finds which may be made

Black-and-white pot lids first appeared in 1840.

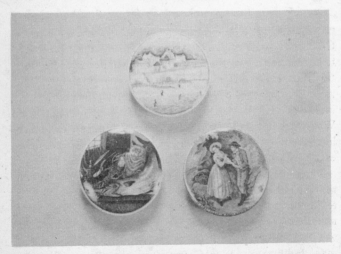

Coloured pot lids were manufactured after 1860 and were intended to be kept, so these are less commonly found.

Commemorative chinaware can form an impressive and varied collection in a relatively short time.

on a dumping ground and are therefore considered to provide the most accurate date of the site's origin. An intriguing task is to be found in dating these articles for it will be discovered that this can be accomplished quite accurately, but simply. The angle at which the bowl slants from the stem provides the best indication, and the shapes of the bowls differ according to age. When first embarking on a collection, one pipe can look much like another, but to those who have knowledge in this field, each small detail will offer a great deal of meaning.

The first clay pipes came into existence in the late sixteenth century in Britain and have changed little in their simple style to this day, when they can still be bought. The method of manufacture was also simple: the bowl was hand moulded in wet clay and often pressed into an iron mould; the stem was made by working the clay over a piece of wire and the two pieces were then joined. Interesting and elaborately shaped bowls were also made, sometimes depicting man or animal heads, in the late nineteenth century.

These decorative pipes do find their way to the dumps, but it is far more common to find the traditional clay pipes which were often smoked only a few times before being discarded. They were once sold at a farthing each, given away by the tobacconist with each purchase, or by publicans to their clients. People would therefore have acquired quite a number of them and tended to throw them away when they became blocked or needed cleaning.

MAKING A COLLECTION

Once the values of finds have been identified, the dump hunter can then make a decision as to what his collection will contain. One of the problems which one faces in this hobby is wondering just what to do with the hundreds of varying dump spoils. Results are rapid, and one soon finds oneself inundated with bottles and other oddments which have been recovered. Many containers can be used, having been thoroughly cleaned or sterilized, for storage in the house and an attractive display of ornaments can be formed. But once one has decided upon the type of article which will make an appealing collection, the most productive method of disposal of unwanted items is to sell or swap them for an item which complements the chosen collection. This can be achieved by frequenting the many auctions held up and down the country, the majority of which are called 'bottle auctions' but they invariably include pot lids, clay pipes and just about every other kind of article one could imagine. In appearance, they are similar to the old flea markets and most enjoyable even if one has no intention of buying, selling or swapping. One visit to such an event will prove that everything and anything which is unwanted for your own collection is saleable.

5

ROCKHOUNDING

Rockhounding as a profession and hobby began several decades ago in North America, probably surviving from the older art of prospecting for gold, but from the Stone Age man has hoarded interesting stones. The fascination of possessing and being able to polish a stone to give it an everlasting finish was discovered in the New Stone Age, when man had learned to grind his tools of flint, obsidian and jade to increase their cutting power and had also noticed that when polished, they became more attractive and pleasing in their appearance. In the eighteenth and nineteenth centuries, fine collections of rocks and minerals were being made, though it was an occupation generally for the wealthy and for scientists who possessed rare knowledge of what they sought. In the Victorian and Regency eras when the seaside holiday industry began, it was fashionable to collect pebbles from the beach to take home as attractive ornaments.

Today it is a pastime which everyone can try, for no matter where one lives, attractive and valuable rocks and minerals are to be found on beaches, around the countryside and even in towns. Although fossils and the occasional attractive rock specimen can command a high price, it is true to say that the value of pebbles is intrinsic rather than financial. The fascination of collecting rocks and pebbles to keep them in their natural state or to polish them and reveal their patterns, colours and permanent brilliance, is one which must be experienced to be believed. The collector or 'rockhound' is rarely content to merely collect; his hobby develops into the making of jewellery and ornaments from his spoils. In Chapter 14 directions and hints for polishing stones are given. In this chapter we are concerned only with the basic knowledge required to commence the hobby.

ROCKS AND MINERALS

Before seeking it is important to understand just what pebbles and rocks are and where they come from, in order to learn and develop the art of identification and appreciation. Firstly, one should understand the difference between rocks and minerals, for pebbles will be found which fall into either category, with the exception of those of organic origin (such as amber and jet). Without entering too deeply into technicalities it can be said that a mineral is a chemical substance which has a fixed composition, whereas a rock may be defined as originating from any of the numerous constituents of the earth's crust. Rock is constructed of varying types and quantities of minerals which originate from the earth's crust and it is the combination of these properties and quantities which segregate rocks into different types. Virtually every rock and mineral type may be found in pebble form, including sapphires, rubies, gold, silver and even diamonds; gemstones, both precious and semi-precious are to be found as pebbles.

THE ORIGIN OF ROCKS

It is easy to glance at a pebble and enjoy it for its attractive appeal, but few people offer them the appreciation they deserve for the journey they have been subject to throughout the ages. The planet we live on was once a fiery ball and all rock was like the molten rock which oozes from a volcano. The earth then cooled, enabling the first rock to be created which is still abundant today. The rocks which originated in this way are called igneous rocks and are one of the three rock types which should be understood by the rockhound. Quartz is one of these igneous rocks.

The next stage in rock formation is the category of the sedimentary rock which has been formed over the years by weathering. The natural agents of erosion worked on the igneous rock breaking particles of it away to form pebbles, mud and sand. Limestone and sandstone are two of the many types of sedimentary rock.

The third type is metamorphic rock which is formed by heat and/or pressure. For instance, this occurs when the state of igneous or sedimentary rock is altered by the presence of a mass of hot magma (a molten stratum under the solid crust of the earth), and its properties are changed to form a new rock type. Marble is a typical metamorphic rock.

BEGINNING A SEARCH

For the beginner, a suitable site on which to commence a search is a pebbled beach, initially using no more equipment than a pocket penknife with a sharp blade and a bag in which to carry rocks and pebbles. The first problem which faces the beginner is knowing just what to collect. The solution to this is simply to collect whatever pebble appeals to the eye or seems intriguing. They may then be taken home and identified or used to experiment with polishing. There are, however, a few basic rules to be remembered which eliminate the possibility of taking home pebbles which are absolutely useless for polishing.

Tumble polishing (see page 172) is when pebbles are placed inside a rotating drum with abrasive grit. This is a popular and efficient method of polishing pebbles and gems and governs the first rule of collecting. Do not be too ambitious with the size of pebbles, for large pebbles do not tumble well and are difficult to use in making jewellery if this is the ultimate aim. The pebbles which will not polish can be noticed, with practice, by their feel and appearance. Porous pebbles such as sandstone are not worthy of collection and, as with all other porous pebbles, it will be noticed that they remain wet far longer than the other pebbles around them. A scrape with the penknife will reveal the fact that they are simply too soft. Most pebbles which are badly cracked or pitted do not deserve the time which will be spent in polishing them and all too often the result is that they fracture further in the process. Pebbles of man-made material also appear in surprising abundance on a beach and here again, the sea proves its ability in the art of camouflage. Pieces of coloured glass appear very attractive though worthless, but brick, porcelain, earthenware and concrete should be discarded. Brick can sometimes be deceptive for it may be mistaken for jasper, though the softness (revealed when scraped with a penknife) will be the deciding factor.

Generally speaking, the best stones to tumble are those which are hard and tough. It is important that one should begin by collecting those pebbles which are attractive, rather than by studying the appearances of gemstones, and searching only for those, for by falling into this trap one soon finds a restricting field in which to work. Searching along the water's edge is the best place to commence and if the sun is shining, the patterns and colour of pebbles will be revealed more easily. When a stone is wet, it is a useful guide as to how it will look when polished.

EQUIPMENT

To avoid the unnecessary problem of taking home too many pebbles, the decision of whether a pebble is worth keeping should be made while on the beach. A penknife may be used to test the hardness of the pebble, to help identify it and to scrape off encrustation through weathering.

A small geologist's hammer may also be used to split stones open for closer examination. Many pebbles turn out to be

Rockhounding equipment: geologist's hammer, magnifying glass, penknife, and unglazed tile for use as a streak plate.

Breaking rocks with a geologist's hammer.

black inside and white outside or black outside and red inside. Ideally, this hammer should have a square head one side and a pick on the other, it should weigh approximately two pounds with a stem of approximately ten inches bound with perforated rubber to absorb some impact. Stonemasons' cold chisels may additionally be used. The hammer may also be used to chip at rocks to remove veins of semiprecious matter which often occur.

A useful guide as to which rock one can expect to find is given in a geological map, obtainable from publishers or the Geological Survey of Great Britain, who produce geological counterparts to the Ordnance Survey maps. This will offer information as to the predominant rock types of the area and therefore assist in the choosing of sites.

A well-equipped collector can also buy or make a testing kit to aid in the identification of his specimens. The conventional kit contains nine metal rods and fixed to their tips are rocks or minerals of known hardness. A convenient and widely accepted system was devised in the nineteenth century by Frederick Mohs and is called the Mohs Hardness Scale which is as follows, beginning with the softest:

1	Talc	6	Feldspar
2	Gypsum	7	Quartz
3	Calcite	8	Topaz
4	Fluorite	9	Corundum
5	Apatite	10	Diamond

Number 6 rod, therefore, will have feldspar set in its tip and if the stone under test is scratched by this rod and none below it, its hardness is 5 as it is softer than feldspar. Most literature lists the hardness of a gemstone according to Mohs' system which renders this system a useful guide in identification. For use while on site as a fairly accurate guide, the following implements may be used:

One's own fingernail: hardness 2

A cupro-nickel coin (such as a ten-pence piece): hardness 3
Glass: hardness 5–5.5
Small steel file: hardness 6.5

It is useful to know that all minerals which exceed hardness 7 are precious stones.

Another generally accepted method of identification is to test the specimen for the colour of its 'streak'. Some minerals have a fairly constant colour, whilst others occur in a wide variety of different colours. For identification purposes it is important to differentiate between the apparent colour and the specimen's real colour which is accomplished by means of the streak. The process is simply to rub the specimen along a streak-plate (a piece of unglazed porcelain) and observe its colour.

A small magnifying glass of about × 10 is useful for observing the crystalline structures of rocks and minerals and this completes the basic items necessary for the identification of rocks and minerals.

SITES

The beach is an ideal site on which to learn the basics of rockhounding, but many more sites await the keen hunter. A quarry, especially where blasting has taken place, offers exciting discoveries. Excavations such as open-cast mining sites or old railway cuttings hold possibilities. Shingle, pebbles and rocks from the beds of rivers also hold great potential. Gravel from driveways and contents from the spoil heaps of building excavation commonly provide attractive stones and semiprecious gems.

PRECIOUS AND SEMIPRECIOUS STONES

Contrary to what one would initially imagine, the British Isles is rich in both precious and semiprecious gems. Listed below are a few of the more important varieties and illustrated is their rough form (as they may be found on a beach, for instance) and their appearance when polished. For a better means of identi-

Rough and polished tiger's eye, a member of the quartz family.

RIGHT: Quartz in rough, polished and faceted form.

Sandrose in natural form. Sandrose is crystallized sand and can be picked up in windswept sandy areas.

Crazy lace agate in
rough and polished
form.

ABOVE: Blue lace agate in rough and
polished form.

Cornelian in rough and
polished form.

fication, their hardness and streak is also listed.

Quartz is the most common mineral, forming twelve per cent of the earth's crust. All the specimens illustrated on page 78 are varieties of the quartz family, their hardness is 7 and streak is colourless, white or grey. This mineral may be found virtually anywhere, but in their crystal form (amethyst or rock crystal) are found especially in cavities of igneous rock.

Amethyst is one of the most sought-after and popular of the quartz family especially in its crystal form. It has a particularly long and rich history in the British Isles, and was once extensively mined in the West Country by the Romans. In the clay pits of Cornwall and around the coast of Redruth, amethyst crystals may be found. Scotland too has its fair share of amethyst to be found among the granite rocks. The amethyst was named by the Greeks who called it *amethystos,* meaning unintoxicating and it was used as a deterrent and remedy for intoxication. The purple colouring of this gemstone varies greatly in shade, but the deeper its colour, the better quality the stone.

Agate is another of Britain's gemstones which may be found in quality, size and quantity, virtually anywhere. Its hardness is 6.5 and streak is colourless, white or grey. Agate is believed to be one of the oldest known minerals, being used for ornamental purposes in 5000 BC. The name of this gem derives from a town now called Dirillo where agates were once mined along the river Achates in southern Sicily. Agates are predominant in central Scotland, Scottish border country, beaches along the east coast particularly in Northumberland and Yorkshire. A walk through the fields of central England also reveals an astounding number of agates, especially on ploughed fields when, after wet weather, these gems will be easily noticed.

Garnet is a popular and decorative gemstone, its hardness is 7 and its streak is colourless. It occurs in igneous and metamorphic rock almost exclusively in the Scottish Highlands, though reports of holidaymakers picking up these stones on beaches around England have occurred.

Serpentine obtains its name from the Latin *serpens* meaning snake, for it was believed to be a deterrent and cure against snake bites. Its hardness is 3–4 and its streak is white. Serpentine occurs in igneous rock and appears in a wide variety of shades of green, sometimes mottled and spotted like a snake's skin.

Cornelian has a hardness of 6.5 and its streak is colourless, white or grey. The colour ranges from red to orange, but the most prized stones are bright orange. They may be found almost anywhere around Britain.

Topaz is a precious stone which has been popular for many years. Its hardness is 8 and its streak is colourless to grey. In Britain, topaz may be found in the Scottish Highlands and Cornwall. The stone typically occurs in cavities in igneous rock and is most commonly colourless, white or grey in appearance.

Emerald has a hardness of 8 and its streak is colourless, white or grey. Emeralds of perfect colour are sometimes held in higher esteem than diamonds and have been popular since ancient times. Emeralds may be found in such desolate areas as Dartmoor and in gravel beds of rivers in the Lake District of England.

Sapphire has a hardness of 9 and its streak is colourless to grey. Scotland has the highest success rate in Britain for the discovery of this stone where it is sought for in burns, especially on the Isle of Arran. The darker the blue of the stone, the more highly prized it is.

6

PROSPECTING

Since time immemorial, gold has been the ultimate in riches, and equally rich are the history and legends which surround it. Surprisingly, therefore, gold is neither the rarest nor the most valuable substance, but its great popularity has rendered it an accepted standard of monetary and commercial value. Like most other minerals, gold is found virtually everywhere in the world but is more predominant in some areas than others.

The first prospectors were believed to have come from Crete, when, before 2000 BC, gold was being mined by the Carpathians. In Roman times, gold was brought from Transylvania, Austria and north-west Spain to Rome in quantities of approximately six and a half tons a year. The major gold rushes in history brought about some drastic changes in civilization. The gold rush in California in 1848 laid the foundations for the USA's economy, and the gold rush in Australia trebled her population in the 1850s. Even Britain had its gold rush days, especially in Scotland where a thirty-five ounce gold nugget was discovered in 1502 which introduced gold mining on behalf of the Crown during the reigns of James IV and James V. In the mid-nineteenth century, prospectors again flocked to Scotland to work the rivers and soil for gold.

Today, prospecting is an astonishingly flourishing activity, though accomplished in its traditionally discreet manner even in more sparsely gold-bearing countries such as Britain. In

Australia, a gold rush in 1978 swept the old gold fields in the West, with both professional and amateur treasure hunters making highly successful discoveries. The majority of these prospectors use metal detectors to locate the gold nuggets, as opposed to the more traditional method of panning. The method has proved highly successful, and their finds are realizing very high prices. Many of the nuggets are being valued not only for their worth as bullion, but also as specimens. A forty-seven ounce nugget, for instance, which was recently discovered by one prospector, was valued at £4,200 for its gold, but as a specimen it was worth £15,000.

One great contributing factor of the new Australian gold rush is the removal of restrictions which, until recently, made it illegal to possess gold. Similarly, in the United States on 31 December 1974, the government relinquished its forty-one year ban on the private ownership of gold. As this date drew close, foreign gold markets prepared themselves in anticipation of high profits in selling gold to the Americans. A disappointment however was in store, for the Americans discovered that they could prospect and find gold for free, enjoying both the search and not having to pay high market prices in order to own the precious substance.

Prospecting for gold in the United States has a long and rich history. The famous 1848–9 gold rush in California, where the principal gold region is about five hundred miles long and about fifty miles broad, following the route of the Sierra Nevada river, averaged approximately one ounce of gold per prospector per day. It is estimated that in those two years, gold worth some £20 million was extracted. The gold which was panned from the rivers in this region was combined with quartz crystal.

Today, treasure hunters in this area are discovering the pleasure and profits of weekend prospecting using the old, but still efficient, method of panning, and that of metal detecting.

THE DISTRIBUTION OF GOLD

The initial consideration for the prospector is to understand how gold is distributed and where it is to be found. Like other minerals mentioned in the previous chapter, this metal is naturally distributed throughout the world. Gold is predominantly found disseminated in quartz veins, but the agents of erosion work on these veins and the gold, because of its high specific gravity, becomes concentrated in secondary deposits of sand or gravel, known as placer (in dry areas) or alluvial (in water) type.

Gold is often found in rivers for when these waters, in forming their routes, broke their way through hills and rocks, the gold which was present in the rocks became subject to constant attrition and was eventually broken into small flakes or dust and conveyed by the current. According to the velocity of the river or stream (and consequently the extent of erosion to which the gold-bearing rocks had been subject), the fineness or coarseness of the gold particle is determined. In more passive rivers, where there is a constant but fairly weak current, the gold may be found in nugget form, similar to pebbles in shape and size.

It has also become a highly productive aspect of prospecting to search in and around old gold-mines, where spoil heaps still contain nuggets which have been missed and the mine floors and walls offer astonishing discoveries, but the use of a metal detector is recommended on this type of site.

RECOGNIZING GOLD

The ability to recognize gold is important, for although this is quite simple once some knowledge of its characteristics is gained, there are a few minerals with which it may be confused. To make matters worse, these minerals tend to occur in the same regions where gold is present. Not surprisingly, these substances have become known as 'fool's gold'. Pyrite and other yellow metallic minerals which can be confused with gold, may be distinguished by their brittle formation. Flakes of mica, which may also be confused with flakes of gold, are not malleable like gold and also differ in that they have a very low specific gravity. Gold has a high specific gravity, 19.28 for pure gold, a hardness of 2.5–3, and the streak is brilliant yellow. More immediately recognizable is its extreme heaviness, its non-tarnishing colour and its malleability. Special testing equipment is available, but seeking the advice of a local museum or other authority is usually adequate.

Getting down to the actualities of prospecting, a mention should be made of the major equipment which is available to assist the prospector and the methods by which they should be employed.

As panning for gold was the first method to be used, and is indeed still used successfully today, this technique will be considered first.

PANNING

A pan is the only piece of equipment necessary to accomplish this method and the implement may be a suitable item of kitchenware or, ideally, a specially manufactured gold pan available from treasure hunting equipment stockists. A plastic pan is best, firstly because of its durability and secondly because the pan is usually used in addition to other techniques and equipment, including a metal detector – which would be unlikely to pick up a gold nugget inside a metal pan! The colour of the pan should be dark to assist in sighting gold amongst its contents, and its depth should be approximately six inches with a twelve-inch diameter.

When a suitable area has been chosen, the method is to fill the pan partially with matter from the river bed, then add sufficient water to cover the contents, allowing time for the contents to become saturated. The larger stones which are seen to be of no value may be discarded before the pan, held level, is submerged so that the water just covers its brim. The pan is

A gold pan.

Panning for gold in an English river.

then rotated back and forth in combination with a gentle rocking motion which allows the mud and clay to flow over the edge until the water in the pan is clear. Remove the pan from the water at this point and remove the smaller pebbles and other items of no worth. Once again, submerge the pan, then gently tilt the nearest edge to an angle of about forty-five degrees with only the front half of the pan submerged in the water. While still continuing gently with the rotating action, slowly increase the tilt to approximately sixty degrees until eventually the only matter left in the pan is the heavier material and, ideally, the gold.

An extension of the idea of panning is the sluice, which consists of a tray with one end open and a hopper at the other. Extending along the tray are rifle boards behind which gold and heavier objects are trapped when material is conveyed to the hopper and sluiced with water.

The traditional type of sluice used for gold panning in the nineteenth-century gold rushes.

USING METAL DETECTORS

On dry land and also in water, metal detectors are used successfully to recover gold, especially in its nugget form. The techniques and approach, however, differ from those of searching in the usual manner with a detector. The areas which offer amounts of gold unfortunately offer a high degree of mineralization in the ground, creating bad ground effect problems. A ground exclusion detector is a distinct advantage, while with other detectors the tuning must be carefully and accurately accomplished to minimize the ground effect.

When using the detector in water to locate gold, care should be taken not to allow the control box to become wet or submerged in the water. It may seem impossible for one to allow this to occur but at the sight of gold anything can happen. The gold pan may be used very successfully in water when combined with the use of a metal detector and a garden trowel. When a signal is obtained, a trowelful or two of earth is taken from that area of the river bed and placed in the plastic pan. A quick sweep over its contents with the detector will reveal whether the metal object is among the contents of the pan. If the object can immediately be seen, so much the better, but otherwise the usual method of panning should be employed to discover the signal's cause.

DREDGING

Dredging can also be used as a method for discovering gold and is quite popular amongst amateur and professional prospectors, especially in the USA. These underwater dredging machines, manufactured in a variety of shapes and sizes, are generally used in working the more concentrated areas of gold deposits. The most productive technique is for the dredger to be used in combination with a metal detector, with a separate operator for each. Areas containing high mineralization are located by the metal detector, whilst the dredger follows behind, sucking up and searching the material from the bed of the location.

PROFITS FROM GOLD

An avid prospecting enthusiast of the recent Australian gold rush (which has been estimated to have resulted in a million dollars being discovered in two years), is Bob Sargent. He has taken up the hobby professionally since his South Australian farm was affected by disease and threatened him with bankruptcy. In 1979, at the height of the gold rush, he had plans to pay off his mortgage in cash and perhaps return to settle there one day, after he has sold the gold he has discovered. His success began when he purchased a new detector and took it for a field test in an area which was reputed to contain gold. His first signal led him to a three and a half ounce gold nugget lying four inches underground. In a very short period he had discovered 560 ounces of gold which was officially priced at $A108,080.

Not every one can be as fortunate as to live in such a generous domain nor be as skilled in prospecting as this man, but the sound advice which he offers can be heeded and used to achieve perhaps more modest successes. He believes that those who strike gold on their first day are just plain lucky, for it usually takes approximately six months of practice, diligent searching, and research into probable locations, before effort is rewarded.

7

DOWSING

Many treasure hunters, in particular metal detector users, have experienced an unexplainable sixth sense while out searching, hunches or intuition which have led them to the discovery of treasure. Since the beginning of time folklore, legends and history have told of apparitions, ghostly voices or omens which involve treasure discoveries. Many of these stories have existed for centuries and, whether they be fact or fantasy, such tales will continue so long as there is treasure to seek.

Most metal detector users have at least one tale to tell of 'feelings' which have led them to a site containing treasure, which in turn has encouraged a great deal of enthusiasm and interest in the subject of dowsing. Many successful treasure hunters rely on dowsing with the use of 'Mexican needles' on maps to locate the area before using a metal detector to locate the precise spot on the ground. In America, many treasure hunters dowse for treasure with high success rates and even in Britain, dowsing societies up and down the country continue to flourish.

This chapter is included in this book firstly because it is a subject which is of obvious interest to the treasure hunter, and secondly because it is a means of finding what one seeks. It is strongly advocated by experts in this field that to be a successful dowser, one must have the 'need to know'. It is beyond coincidence that greater success is achieved by those who genuinely have a need to experience the art, than by those motivated only by the creation of personal riches. The following account of the techniques and application of dowsing includes the basic knowledge necessary to commence and will enable anyone to decide whether dowsing works for them.

USING THE SUBCONSCIOUS

Dowsing is the ability to find objects by use of the subconscious mind. It is a faculty possessed by all, although developed and acknowledged by few. The techniques are simple, though metaphysical. The applications of dowsing are numerous and, once learnt, the technique is advantageous throughout life to its master and to others. Some of its applications include the finding of water (also known as water divining), minerals and precious stones, any object lost by oneself or by others, sunken ships beneath the sea, caves and tunnels underground, ancient burial sites, and even missing people. Dowsing societies constantly receive requests for all such assignments, most of which are successfully achieved. Farmers most commonly employ the art for detection of underground water; the building industry has used it to detect unforeseen characteristics beneath a site such as water, cables, cellars, caves, drains, etc.; archaeologists for detecting ancient sites and remains; even the police have occasionally employed the art to recover missing items and people.

The question which will be asked by the sceptic, is, 'How does it work?' and the answer to those who have absolutely no faith is that it will not. Scepticism immediately forms an impenetrable mental barrier to much that can be learnt and for this reason one should remain open-minded to everything. Science has not yet accepted the art of dowsing, for it cannot be given a scientific description of how it works but, nevertheless, many scientists are dowsers and most others cannot deny that it does work. A demonstration of the art is often the only way to convince the sceptic.

Few individuals today understand very much of their sub-conscious mind or, indeed, allow themselves to get to know it. The conscious mind, which toils throughout the day dealing with problems and situations, often receives messages from the subconscious which too often we choose to ignore. Intuition and instinct come from the subconscious mind. Everyone at some time experiences this sixth sense but few rarely take the time to encourage more such occurrences. Dowsing is one method of using and developing a better understanding of the subconscious mind, with the added advantage of being able to recover lost items.

DOWSING EQUIPMENT

Dowsing may be used to recover items lost by other people and by oneself, regardless of their value in intrinsic or monetary terms, or where, when and how they have been lost. There are, however, some implements which assist the dowser better than others, according to their application. To illustrate this point, the example of Mrs Y. Knowles of Kent may be used. Mrs Knowles began dowsing in 1975 and had only been developing the art for two months when she decided to apply it to the recovery of a long-lost charm bracelet which was of great sentimental value. The bracelet had been lost in 1967, whilst she was on a ten-mile sponsored walk, and the bracelet could have been lost at any point during the walk. The first technique she used was that of map dowsing, incorporating the use of a pendulum and a large scale Ordnance Survey map. Having obtained a positive response in a certain area on the map she then visited the site and this time used angle rods to locate the exact position. A positive response was received beneath the boughs of a sycamore tree and after digging in the soil, only an inch or two away from where the signal had been received, the bracelet was found just four inches beneath the soil.

Before explaining the techniques used with different pieces

The correct way to hold angle rods for divining water.

of equipment, it must be emphasized that they are merely media to assist the dowser. They work on the principle that when the subconscious mind feels the presence of what is being sought, it sends an impulse similar to a reflex action through the body which is measured and made apparent by movement of the equipment held in the hand. There is no magic in the actual implements used; they are merely a means of measuring the signal.

Pendulums may be as simple or as complex and extravagant as one wishes. They are merely a weight, suspended on a length of string with no stipulations regarding weight and size except that they should be able to swing easily and not be so light that they are extensively affected by wind when being used in the open. Pendulums for use with map dowsing should have a point at the end for greater accuracy. For the thread on which the pendulum swings, a length should be chosen which is comfortable to work with when sitting and holding it above a map, and it should be of a fibre which does not cause the pendulum to spin as does a twisted fibre. The more elaborate, custom-made pendulums are manufactured so that the pendulum top unscrews to reveal a hollow inside which a related piece or example of the sought-after substance may be placed (for instance, a small piece of gold to find a gold ring).

Angle rods are found to be most successful for the beginner but they are also used by professionals. These again may be kept as simple or elaborate as one wishes. A most popular implement being used today is the wire coat hanger which is cut into two rods with a right angle bend in each, as shown on the previous page. A rod is held in either hand, and kept parallel to each other until the presence of the sought-after substance is indicated by the rods turning inwards or crossing over each other.

V rods are traditionally depicted in reference to the water diviner. This method may be used for any application in dowsing; the rods are traditionally made of hazel twigs but also apple wood, nylon and whalebone. These can be purchased from treasure hunting stockists. The main concern when considering material is that it should be of a slightly pliable substance to withstand tension. The length of the rod may be anything between six inches and two feet in length, though professional dowsers commonly use twelve inch rods. The V rod is easily made by choosing two rods, preferably of the same diameter and length, and binding them together at one end firmly.

There are other tools which the dowser can use, but the above three are the basic ones and it is advantageous to keep tools simple and to a minimum when beginning. It must be remembered that dowsing is a personal matter and one should therefore experiment to discover tools which are suitable both for the task and the user.

METHODS OF USE

A code to work by is imperative, for this enables the subconscious mind to relate to and translate its findings into something which the conscious mind can comprehend. The following code is only one way but is the most popular amongst experienced dowsers.

When using the pendulum for indoor work such as map dowsing, hold it in one hand, between the finger and thumb, over the map. A positive response is an anti-clockwise movement and a negative response is a clockwise movement. The direction of the sought-after item may also be determined by feeling which way the pendulum is 'pulled'. Similarly, when being used in the field, the direction may be signified by a pull and responses are also signified by the same code.

Angle rods are usually used for outdoor work and they are normally held parallel to each other; maintain a firm hold on their short sections so that they point away from the body. The positive response is when the rods turn inwards and lie parallel against the body. The direction for the search is determined as the rods begin to turn inwards.

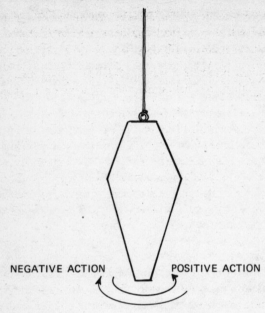

NEGATIVE ACTION   POSITIVE ACTION

Positive and negative reactions with the pendulum method.

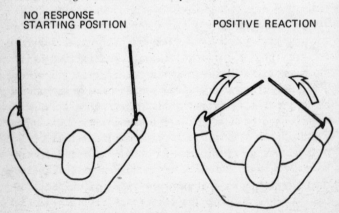

NO RESPONSE
STARTING POSITION   POSITIVE REACTION

Positive and negative reactions with angle rods.

The V rod is held so that the palms of the hands face upwards and the fingers wrap around the rods, with the pointed end being slightly higher than the level of the hands. When the find is made the tip points down, towards the ground.

THE ART OF DOWSING

It has been mentioned that everyone is capable of dowsing though, as with most other aspects of life, some people are more suited and more successful in this art than others and the only way to discover one's capabilities is to try. It is not uncommon for a person to discover success on the first trial, though generally speaking, practice is needed. An ability in the art of concentration is an asset, but more important is the gift, or development, of relaxation. Concentration without relaxation tends to form a barrier which cannot easily be penetrated by messages from the subconscious.

To adopt the correct frame of mind for use when dowsing, and to gain a better understanding of the difference between the conscious and subconscious mind, the following exercise is most useful. Sit relaxed, but not in a lazy position, and allow yourself to become merely the onlooker of the thoughts which pass through the mind, only noticing but not pursuing them. The less thoughts which appear, the better, and one will soon be able to get into the necessary state of mind for dowsing, which is to be relaxed with the mind as empty as is possible.

It is important to keep work simple when beginning, and it has been found that most people find dowsing for water comes most naturally. This may perhaps be a form of instinct, similar to the instinct which informs animals of the locations of waterholes where they may drink. As with all other applications of dowsing, these aspects of intuition and instinct are inherent in everyone and, although used to their fuller potential in former times when the necessity was greater, these senses have become dormant in modern man through lack of exercise. To develop this forgotten sixth sense, some simple exercises may be used, such as working over one's own house to find water pipes and drains or experimenting by asking another person to bury a bottle of water beneath the soil. One may then progress to objects of various metals and then specific objects, such as a bunch of keys.

When some experience has been gained, one is then able to apply it to proper tasks, such as items one has lost in the past. It will be discovered that these tasks develop with surprising ease, for once again there is the 'need' which always encourages better results. The more that is known about the sought-after object, the better, and it is for this reason that some dowsers find greater accuracy through placing a piece of related material in the pendulum. Similarly, when map dowsing, some prefer to hold a related item in one hand, a piece of Roman pottery, for instance, if looking for an item of Roman origin.

Dowsing as a method of searching for lost or hidden substances is an art which has been with us for many years, and will no doubt continue to exist regardless of the scepticism it tends to arouse. It is improbable that it will ever be accepted as an undisputed fact that dowsing works, but certainly a great number of people are becoming interested in it and using its applications all the time. The decision of whether dowsing does or does not work should therefore be a personal one, and until one tries – who knows?

8
THE SEA

Having a knowledge of the methods of various ways of treasure hunting, the searcher may then commence applying them to particular sites. The next few chapters are concerned with specific types of sites and the rewards they offer.

When considering the vast and varied treasures of the sea, we should first look to the past. It is a general rule for the treasure hunter whose interests lie in beachcombing or metal detecting, that the most extensively-used areas are where discoveries are to be made. The beaches of our past were very sparsely populated, unlike the appearance they adopt today, but rich and ancient treasures are nevertheless to be found. Although few people lived around or frequented the beaches, the activities which did occur usually involved treasure in one form or another.

WRECKING

Although the majority of coastal inhabitants were desperately poor, most of them owned small boats for such purposes as fishing, smuggling, wrecking or salvaging. Apart from fishing, these activities all involved the transportation or recovery of treasure with the inevitable result of losses either in the sea or on the shore. Wrecking was a lucrative occupation for many coastal inhabitants, particularly in conjunction with smuggling and piracy, and a great number of people were involved in it well into the nineteenth century.

The wreckers relied on distressed shipping as a means of survival and the more treacherous their coastline, the better the pickings. Navigational aids were few at that time and seamen had to rely on sighting land before being able to take their bearings. This meant that the vessel had to come dangerously close to the shore, especially in foggy weather, and risk going aground. Wreckers would sometimes use lights to lure ships to their peril, so that they could fulfil their task of plundering the cargo. The trade of 'hovelling' was equally lucrative and involved the recovery of ships' anchors and cables which could later be sold at a high price to other ships who had lost such items.

On coasts where richly-laden shipping was notorious, there would be a mad scramble when a ship was seen to be in distress. All the local boatmen would rush to the scene, often in more than a hundred small craft, but few had any interest in helping survivors for purely humane reasons. In the sixteenth century, law decreed that a vessel could not be classed as a wreck as long as it had a survivor aboard. For many, this was an open invitation to murder survivors, or at least offer no assistance while they were drowning, but for others, interest lay in the recovery of survivors and some cargo which would result in a salvage reward.

Whatever the case, shipwreck was a lucrative proposition and often the only form of income for these people. While conveying bounty from the site of the ship to the shore and up the beach to their homes or hideouts, a great deal would have been lost in their haste. For the metal detecting enthusiast and beachcomber, it is therefore well worth investigating the routes that these people took, and the secret paths used by smugglers.

SALVAGING
The old practice of wrecking is only one small aspect of the vast treasures which can be obtained from sunken ships. The

A fossilized shark's tooth is discovered while rockhounding.

Searching the shore line in the vicinity of an ancient building should yield objects dating back to the time when the site was a thriving community.

word 'treasure' immediately conjures up pictures of the Spanish Main, pirates, sea-chests of gold and tropical islands, but Britain has a coast as rich in treasure as anywhere in the world, with an estimated 200,000 shipwrecks. The Spanish Armada, in its attempt to invade England in 1588, contributed to this figure, as did the First and Second World Wars and the terrific hurricane of 1859 which sent many ships to their doom. Many of the vessels which foundered round the coastline of the British Isles had cargoes of bullion or other exotic treasures which have become a well-established part of history and folklore.

For many years it has been thought that underwater treasure hunting for these riches is the prerogative of only a privileged few. But for someone with the determination and ability for organization, together with a small financial outlay and, above all, a respect for our heritage, the rewards are there. Diving training is imperative, and for a modest price, in comparison to the potential return, underwater metal detectors are also available.

All sunken ships, however, do have an owner, be it the Crown, the country of origin or the country in whose waters it sank. Salvage rights may be owned by a private person or company. It is therefore of great importance, if one is to avoid disappointment, expense and legal liability, that the proper authorities be approached before considering a search. In British waters, salvage rights have to be obtained, at a fee, from the Admiralty and all discoveries have to be promptly reported to the Receiver of Wrecks. Careful planning and long hours of research are necessary. It is far better to suffer a disappointment while on land and researching through archives, than after an expensive underwater exploration has been undertaken. Although our predecessors had little equipment to help them reap the rewards of treasure ships, they had the determination which in some way or another equipped them with the means to recover an astonishing amount.

It is encouraging to remember that the discoveries of many treasure ships were made by those who began as amateurs, equipped only with the will to succeed. Rex Cowan, a London solicitor who discontinued his profession and devoted his attention to wreck hunting, discovered in 1971 the treasures of the Dutch ship *Hollandia* which foundered on Gunner Rock, Cornwall, in 1743 containing a rich sum of the famous 'pieces of eight'. Soon after the *Hollandia* had sunk, attempts were made by the Dutch East India Company to salvage the coins but although her position was located, the divers were unable to dive the twenty fathoms of water under which she lay. Over two centuries later, after three years of preparation and careful research, Rex Cowan and his team salvaged the treasures of the *Hollandia*. Amongst other beautiful and valuable treasures were literally thousands of Spanish silver hammered cob coins. A proportion of the treasure was sold at auction in 1972 at Sotheby's and realized over £32,000.

BEACHCOMBING

Even for the land-bound treasure hunter who feels more at home beachcombing, shipwrecks still donate their wealth. In fact it has often been the case that the recovery of treasures from the beach have encouraged a diving expedition and assisted the location of a wreck. Near Gunwalloe on the Cornish coast, a treasure ship is now under investigation following local tales that, after stormy seas, housewives used to collect valuable coins in shopping baskets. Two treasure ships have been wrecked close to this point, carrying gold and jewellery, and it has become known as Dollar Cove; and coins are still washed ashore to this day.

It is true to say, however, that the majority of treasures for the beachcomber and metal detector user, are in the form of modern artefacts with only the occasional recovery from a sunken ship's treasure. Most of the coins one may find will date back to the Victorian era, but rough or stormy seas may reveal older ones. It is not unusual to discover a hundred coins an hour after stormy seas and, when a glory hole has been located, jewellery too may be found in astonishing abundance. It is here that the rule for success does apply – the areas in which people have congregated are where the finds are to be made. Areas such as refreshment stalls, piers, changing areas, deck-chair spots, fishing and bathing areas, etc., should all be observed in the summer months. The area above the high tide must also be considered in this category, for it is here that many people stay in order to avoid an incoming tide.

After a storm or particularly rough seas, the beachcomber and metal detector user must work quickly to discover the treasure areas before the items are reclaimed by the sea or, more commonly, covered by the sand with the next tide. The metal detector user should, for this reason, employ different techniques than in his normal search methods. Instead of making a very thorough search of one area before moving on, a fairly quick search should be made in one general direction, for instance the high tide line, until a coin or similarly valuable item is discovered and then a very thorough search should be made of that area. The beachcomber also uses this method after a storm, though his eyes are the only equipment he uses. This has the obvious disadvantage that he only discovers items exposed on the surface, but he has two advantages in that he can work with more speed and probably locate the productive areas or glory holes before the metal detector user, and is able to see immediately whether an object is a bottle top or a coin, instead of having to spend time digging it up. Mrs Creasey of Lincolnshire recently discovered a beautiful gold bracelet, believed to be AD 1000, while she was looking for shells. The bracelet was literally sticking out of the sand and was probably deposited there by the rough seas of the autumn equinox. Whatever the method one uses, the conditions offered after a storm should be well exploited, making use of all the available time one has by knowing in advance the times of the tides.

Len Thompson, successful treasure hunter, concentrates on areas used by holiday-makers to shelter from the wind.

A beautiful tenth-century gold bracelet picked up on the beach by Kay Creasey.

Beachcombing and metal detecting, however, are not restricted only to the period after strong seas, though admittedly one has to work a great deal longer to reap the same rewards as can be found under these conditions; on a calm day, more thorough searches may be made and a much better understanding of the beach acquired. Mrs Green, the proprietor of a treasure hunting shop in Cardiff, discovered, together with three other metal detector users, 2,500 coins in only forty-five minutes, which were not directly the result of a storm. Mrs Green decided to make a thorough search in a glory hole for all the older treasures which had come to reside there from the stormy seas over the years. By digging down a number of feet she discovered that layers or steps of coins existed, each divided by a layer of sand which had built up over the years by the stormy sea depositing the coins and then the calmer seas covering them with sand.

It is not only sea-deposited treasures which follow this pattern, for in some areas this happens with items which are lost and sink far enough to avoid the sea's action. Coins tend to sink quite rapidly until they reach the hardpack. It is a useful and usually very productive exercise to dig a small trench to reach this layer and then use a metal detector to locate the treasures. This method is often used under a pier where much jewellery and coins, dating back to Victorian days, would have been lost, especially if the pier is constructed with open planks.

DUMP DIGGING BY THE SEA

For the dump digger too, there are treasures to be found, especially if his interest lies in the collecting of pot lids. One of the main amusements of the Victorian holiday-maker was to stroll along the promenade eating potted shrimps. Other fish and meat pastes were also sold and when the contents were consumed, the beautifully painted pot lids were discarded in the nearest litter container which eventually found its way to the dump. This dump would not have been far from the beach

Actress Linda Allen (*right*) discusses underwater metal detecting techiques with Kate Johnson, who is holding a metal detector specially designed for underwater use.

but in an area which was inconspicuous to the holiday-makers. Victorian dumps have often been located in areas such as sand dunes or land immediately behind the beach. Pieces of broken glass and pottery may sometimes be seen as a hint to the presence of a dump but clues are also given by the type of vegetation growing. On a seaside dump, tall healthy reeds are the most usual plants to find favourable conditions in the nutrients provided by the dumps.

ROCKS AND MINERALS
Excellent training ground for the rockhound may be found on a beach, a site which is often preferred by professionals too. Searching along the low tide line on a sunny day will display the pebbles' colours at their best and better enable one to recognize the semiprecious stones.

Amber may quite commonly be picked up on a beach and is an item which was not mentioned in Chapter 5 (on rockhounding) for it does not fit into the category of rock or mineral. Nevertheless, amber is a highly sought-after and popular item which can be polished and used in jewellery like any precious and semiprecious stone. Amber dates back to before the Ice Age and is the solidified gum from a species of pine tree called *Pinus succinifera*. The most prized amber specimens have insects trapped inside them which can be seen in the clear amber as perfect as they were when alive before the Ice Age.

The Baltic coast is renowned for amber and has a particularly long and rich history of discoveries. It may be found in Britain also and although, generally speaking, pieces are fairly small they are nevertheless suitable for jewellery. There have been exceptions to this rule, however, such as the block of amber which was found in the early 1900s on a Suffolk beach, which weighed thirteen pounds and sold for £4,500. The Kentish and Norfolk coasts also offer amber more frequently than other areas. It is usually found along and above the high tide line. The shade of amber varies from clear to rich yellow, pink and deep red; the darker the specimen, the more valuable it is.

SAFETY

No matter what type of treasure one seeks, personal safety should not be ignored while engrossed in the search. The advancing tide should always be considered in relation to an available exit, or yet another possession could be taken by the sea.

9
INLAND WATERWAYS

The vast amount and variety of discoveries which await the enthusiastic treasure hunter on our many and varied waterways is limitless. Whether the waters be tidal or non-tidal, wide, narrow, shallow or deep, river beds and surrounding areas are an inexhaustible source of finds. The history of these waterways are long and rich for water has been an essential part of man's existence since time began. Thus for the treasure hunter with a metal detector or for the dump digger, rockhound and prospector, waterways provide rewarding and enjoyable sites.

Before discussing the methods and potential for each hobby, however, an understanding should be gained of the river's distribution pattern, for whether one's treasure is coins and trinkets, clay pipes and bottles, gemstones or gold nuggets, if they are sought actually in the water, then they will all conform to this natural pattern. In the same way that the sea sorts items, so does the river in a far more predictable and less complex way. Hot spots or glory holes occur along a river's path as they do on a beach, but some rivers are far more productive than others, according to what the treasure hunter wishes to search for, and this is a matter which should be decided first.

THE LIFE OF A RIVER

A river's life is divided into three stages; the youthful stage, the middle age stage, and the old age stage. The youthful stage is usually found in higher land and is close to the river's source. The water is very swift flowing and direct in its course, carrying most articles in its flow, depositing only the larger rocks and heavier stones. Items carried do not include coins and most other treasures which the metal detector user seeks, but sometimes include gold nuggets and many other gemstones which are heavier and are dragged along by the current until they reach an obstruction or an area where the current is weaker. The youthful stage therefore is favourable to the prospector and rockhound.

The middle age stage of a river is usually deep and slower in its flow, depositing smaller, but still fairly heavy, material weighing less than coins and rings. Gold panning is sometimes undertaken in this region but the water's depth renders the site undesirable for most treasure hunting other than dredging.

The old age stage is towards the end of a river's life, before it joins the sea. It is slow flowing, relatively shallow, weak in current and often has a pebbled and silt bed - all of which constitute good metal detecting and rockhounding ground. It should be remembered however, that for the moment we are concerned only with the actual river bed and not the banks, for favourable metal detecting and dump digging areas are to be found along each of the river's stages, particularly by the middle and old age stages where habitation occurs.

WHERE TO SEARCH

So, bearing these points in mind and having chosen a suitable stretch of water, the treasure hunter should then commence his study to determine where the possible hot spots occur. Very basically, the most productive areas to search are obstructions, bends, shallow water and eddies. An obstruction, even if it is submerged, will cause a swift turbulence of water, called an

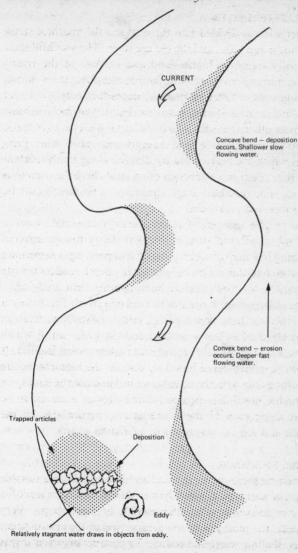

CURRENT

Concave bend — deposition occurs. Shallower slow flowing water.

Convex bend — erosion occurs. Deeper fast flowing water.

Trapped articles

Deposition

Eddy

Relatively stagnant water draws in objects from eddy.

The distribution of articles on the bed of a river.

eddy. This eddy distributes any matter which it draws in to a patch of fairly stagnant water which lies close to it. Obstructions which occur at right angles to the river's flow are also worth searching as they trap many objects which have been dragging along the river's bed. Both sides of the obstruction merit a search, for the eddies often tend to carry matter away from in front of the obstruction and deposit it behind the obstruction where the current is weaker. The bends of rivers are productive sites; the golden rule to remember here is that a river's current erodes from the convex bend (outer bank) and deposits on the concave (inner bank). On the concave bend, the water will be shallower and the current too weak to convey the larger articles it carries.

METAL DETECTING IN WATERWAYS

Metal detecting in and around Britain's waterways is a rewarding adventure which may be experienced by any metal detector owner. For searching in the water, the only additional piece of equipment required is a floating sieve. This may be made by placing a plastic garden sieve in an inflated car tyre inner tube, with a weighted line attached to prevent it floating downstream. A garden trowel is also needed to convey matter from the river bed where the signal has been obtained to the floating sieve. This technique soon develops into a rapid method of retrieving finds.

Once the potential for searching rivers has been realized, choosing a suitable stretch of water can be a fascinating task. Features along the river bank are the best guide to follow when choosing a site along the course of any waterway; footbridges, historical buildings, old ferry sites, mills and weirs are bound to be good starting-points.

Taking the example of a footbridge, consider the possibilities which this site may offer. Footbridges are quite commonly built on the same site as older bridges and if they date back to Roman days, they would have seen the old custom

The floating sieve in use while metal detecting in the shallows of a river.

Michael Cain searches a river bank with a metal detector which has a belt-mounted control box and separate search head.

of travellers throwing a coin into the river for a safe crossing. Such a footbridge may also have been used by the traveller who endeavoured to cross the swollen river with his horse-drawn cart laden with all his possessions or goods for market, which then fall prey to the swift river current.

CANALS AS A SOURCE OF TREASURE

The old canal waterways have proved to be a most rewarding site for metal detecting. Malcolm Hill of Winchester discovered a beautiful solid silver communion set consisting of a chalice, wafer tray and cruet, buried twelve inches below the towpath of the Itchin Navigation Canal. The set has been identified as a sick communion set which was taken by the priest to the homes of people who were ill or disabled. One can only guess at how or why it was lost or concealed on this canal towpath, but it only goes to prove that almost any kind of treasure may be discovered on a canal site.

The Chesterfield Canal was recently the subject of jovial controversy when it was accidentally drained by someone pulling out the plug. Metal detector users took advantage of the event by searching the canal bed and discovered an assortment of valuables including several gold sovereigns. Examples of the variety of treasures which occur in the canals can also be seen by visiting one of the many canal museums. There is rising interest in the restoration of these canals and voluntary organizations have been formed who undertake the dredging of them to remove underwater hazards before reopening them as navigable waterways which may be used for leisure, sport and travel. Many items have been recovered in the process: jewellery, valuable coins, canal tokens, canal company seals, bottles, pot lids, etc. to the extent that special museums have been dedicated to the Canal Age.

Industry and agriculture used the canals for transport extensively between 1700 and 1860, but the waterways of the Fens were used as early as the fourteenth century. After the

Roger Johnson discovers a coin on the edge of a river.

Following disused canal towpaths is a lucrative source of Victorian coins and objects.

coming of the railway in the early nineteenth century, which discouraged many industrial waterway vessels, the canals were used for pleasure rides and holiday-makers. In the mid-nineteenth century they were especially popular for Sunday school outings and even today, barge holidays on the old canals are an attraction. So the canal have seen an abundance of activity which constitutes good metal detecting ground, particularly at places where canal boats were moored.

When searching the towpaths beside the canals, one should search a width of at least five feet, as this was the minimum width used by the gangs of men or the horses who pulled the barges. Mills and weirs are features which merit particular attention for it is here that much money used to change hands. Payment had to be made by the bargemaster to the mill owner or 'wharfinger' before access was permitted, with the inevitable result of coins at some time being dropped into the relentless water or mud in the process.

DUMP DIGGING BY WATERWAYS

Dump digging on riverside locations can prove to be a particularly good site for the hobby, for extensive dumping occurred here in the Victorian era and before. For one of the reasons for this, we can again look back to the Canal Age, when vast amounts of clay were extracted from areas along river banks to construct the waterway system. This left dangerously large holes which were utilized and later concealed by the process of rubbish dumping. Expansion and improvement of the canal system lasted a very long time and throughout its duration, the process of filling in holes with household refuse continued.

The second major reason as to why many dumping sites are found at riversides is again waterway construction. The Victorians were responsible for a great deal of the artificial embankments which were built to change the course of rivers in order to prevent flooding, to reclaim land or to assist

A patch of reeds on a raised river bank indicates the existence of dump.

irrigation for agriculture. The building of an embankment required a great deal of material which had to be cheap, easily
available, and efficient in blocking the water's flow. One
substance could satisfy all these requirements – household
rubbish. The scheme was implemented over the course of
many years, often with a series of embankments being constructed. In each case, many tons of rubbish would have been
transported either by horse-drawn cart or by barge and then
wheelbarrow. Discovering the precise sites of these riverside
dumps is accomplished by research (which will be explained in
Chapter 13) and by observation. Once again, nature provides
some tell-tale clues of the dump's presence by characteristic
vegetation. Reeds, tall healthy nettles, brambles and elder trees
flourish on the well-drained soil which the dump provides.
Pieces of glass and pottery may also be evident on the surface.

For those interested in the collection of clay pipes, these are often to be found beside canal bridges, on the banks near riverside public houses and beside landmarks where canal people would leisurely partake of a pipe whilst watching the barges pass and conversing with friends.

Another possible discovery for the dump digger is a 'witch bottle' that might be found along the course of a river. These bottles are of great historical and collectable value. They were often floated downstream as a prevention against or deflection of witchcraft. They usually took the form of Bellarmine jugs and contained such items as finger-nail cuttings, human hair, pins, and sometimes heart shapes cut from felt and pierced with pins.

GOLD PROSPECTING IN WATERWAYS

Prospecting for gold in rivers is an ancient practice, even in Britain. Great quantities have been obtained from Scotland, Wales, Ireland and, to a lesser degree, from England. The minor gold rush which occurred in 1868 in the Highlands of Scotland was said to earn prospectors about £1 per day when gold was plentiful. The gold was panned from the burns in the Kildonan area and the amount of gold which discoverers reported to the authorities was worth approximately £12,500, a handsome sum in those days. When competition became too great, many other rivers were investigated by prospectors of Scotland, with successful results. Refused permission from farmers, however, they discontinued their ventures and many of these waterways still contain that gold. The Kildonan area has not yet been exhausted especially if one combines panning with the modern advantage of metal detecting.

Wales too, has a rich and plentiful history of gold. The gold from the Dolgellau Hills has been used to make wedding rings and regalia for royalty. County Wicklow in Ireland also had its gold rush days, when prospectors worked a river known as Gold Mines Stream for the precious metal.

The solid silver communion set discovered by Malcolm Hill under the towpath of the Itchin Navigation Canal.

Kate Johnson displays a half-crown found on a river bank.

The youthful stage of a river is most productive in gold, where it will be found close to its source. Research is of major importance when searching for a gold-bearing river. One should endeavour to investigate the local history of where gold has been discovered in the past. A geological map is of assistance in this work. Many prospectors sight promising locations by observing the soil types in the river banks and discover that reddish-brown gravel (which indicates iron oxide) is a hopeful sign of the presence of gold.

ROCKHOUNDING IN WATERWAYS

Rockhounding may also be achieved by panning in rivers or merely by searching the pebbles and rocks along the river banks. The type or stage of river which should be searched varies according to the type of gemstone one seeks so that, generally speaking, any river, regardless of its life stage, will prove rewarding for the rockhound who does not hunt for a specific substance. In the fast-flowing streams and tributaries of a river's youthful stage, sapphires and pearls may be found, especially in Scotland. In the middle age and old age river stages in England, emeralds may be found in river gravels. Of the more common rocks and minerals, such as the agate and quartz families, quantities may be found among gravel beds of rivers virtually anywhere.

10
HIGHWAYS AND BYWAYS

Astonishing numbers of coins, jewellery and other artefacts have been discovered along the highways and byways used to transport people and merchandise. The reason for this success is that the paths and trackways which form an intricate web over the country date back hundreds, sometimes thousands, of years and have been used by an endless variety of folk for different purposes. Royalty, aristocrats, travelling merchants, peasants, vagabonds and thieves, have all used our pathways and consequently a long and rich history has evolved around them.

LEY LINES
Dating the origin of a particular track is difficult. Probably the best clues are to be found in the actual finds retrieved on a site by the metal detector user. Without doubt, many of the old tracks in existence today date back to the early days of ancient Britain. The mysterious routes and intersections of ancient 'ley lines' are an intriguing subject for both the historian and the treasure hunter. Research into the locations of treasure discoveries in relation to ley lines has produced a number of similarities beyond the scope of coincidence. Philip Connolly's hoard of coins was discovered at the intersection of two leys, as was a Hampshire hoard of sovereigns. Many other ancient treasures have been discovered on the path of a ley line which

might lead one to believe that the ley system is indeed a key to the early trackways used by man.

The theory behind ley lines is, simply, that sites of ancient importance align perfectly to form a straight path; where one or more ley lines cross a place of ancient religious significance will often be discovered. To test the theory of the leys, one can take any Ordnance Survey map, preferably of one inch to a mile scale, and draw a circle round all the obviously ancient sites: religious buildings, earthworks, hill forts, castles, tumuli (barrows), standing stones and stone circles. Unless a map of a modern built-up area has been chosen, it will be found that alignments may be made of three or more sites over about ten miles. Using a ruler to mark these alignments, notice that the points form a perfectly straight line running directly through the places of traditional sanctity. By going a step further and actually visiting the site to trace the ley line, further confirmation of its presence will begin to appear, such as markstones, copses, mounds, sightings on hilltops in the direct path of the ley, or sections of old tracks which still remain.

Alfred Watkins, who rediscovered the system of the leys in the 1920s, believed them to be early man's trackways, dating back thousands of years. Proof of the age of these paths can be gauged from the age of the sites marked on the leys. Stonehenge, for instance, is the point where many ley lines stretching far across England intersect.

For the treasure hunter with a metal detector, an interesting and productive project may be found in ley hunting, for it is not uncommon for an ancient congregational point to be discovered on a ley line, where there is no man-made building or other evidence on the map. A compass is a useful addition to equipment and a regular survey of the land while searching will indicate the most potential areas. A word of warning, however, regarding the combination of leys and treasure hunting: most of the monuments, religious buildings and earthworks are archaeological sites where the general public

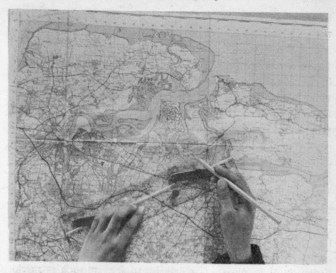

Plotting ley lines with the help of a map.

Derek Ingram following a woodland path. He has discovered over five hundred rings in three years.

Jeremy de Monfalcoln (*right*) and Harry King display their sovereigns and guineas after the treasure trove inquest.

are prohibited from any form of digging and those who do are liable to be severely fined and/or imprisoned.

The tracks leading to the sites, unless in the immediate vicinity, are probably quite legitimate treasure hunting sites.

EXISTING TRACKS

Highways and byways in existence today may well date back to the days of travelling merchants, stage coaches and highwaymen. An important point to remember when metal detecting along these footpaths, is that travellers were often obliged to carry a lot of money and valuables with them. Banks were not in existence until the late eighteenth century and even then were used by only a privileged few. Commercial banks appeared in London at the beginning of the nineteenth century, but not in country districts nor for the general public until fifty years later. So a traveller's financial possessions were

A selection of the rare coins they found in a copse outside Winchester.

either carried on his person or, at times of danger, temporarily buried. Common hiding places were just off the path by a large tree or similar landmark so the spot could be easily recognized for collection.

WOODS AND COPSES

Many coin hoards have been found in woods or copses, just on the outskirts of towns and a little off the beaten track. This is due to an ancient precaution travellers used before entering a town whereby they would temporarily hide their belongings and recover them only when they had established that the inhabitants were trustworthy or when their business was complete. Many of course fell prey to some tragedy, and never recovered their wealth. One such hoard of ninety-seven gold sovereigns and guineas has recently been discovered in a copse just outside Winchester by two fifteen-year-old boys with metal detectors, Jeremy de Montfalcoln and Harry King. The hoard was buried between three large distinctive trees which formed a triangle; the hoard owner must have carefully chosen the spot for easy identification.

One can never be too ambitious when searching a site such as this, for a hoard may be awaiting discovery almost anywhere beside the footpath. The most successful method of determining where a traveller's hoard may lie is to imagine oneself to be the traveller and consider the factors which constitute a safe place to conceal your wealth. Take into consideration the type of soil. Rocky ground would have been difficult for the hoard owner to dig into but crevices would prove adequate. The point at which an old town is sighted from the footpath should also be considered, as should the amount of cover a particular site offers from prying eyes.

SPECIAL TREES

As with all treasure hunting sites, finds are not evenly distributed and the course of a footpath is no exception. Prospective hoard-hunting areas have been discussed but many other features along a highway or byway deserve particular attention, apart from the more obvious ones such as old fallen trees, stiles and streams. The significance of each type of old tree should be known to the treasure hunter, for many once involved rituals concerning the sacrifice of money or the traditional concealment of valuables. The well-known saying 'money doesn't grow on trees' is frequently being proved wrong by treasure hunters who have gained some knowledge of tree lore, and used it to hunt for treasures. Tree lore was common in ancient Britain; not only were there 'mile trees' (from which over a third of Britain's place names are derived), but boundary trees, toll trees, marker trees, parliament or 'tort' trees, centre-of-forest trees and many more. Most of these had a footpath leading to them or were chosen along the course of an existing footpath. Each of these trees has a history like a character of its own, being used as a rendezvous for huntsmen, pedlars, travellers, smugglers, royalty, lovers and so on, thus providing an infallibly productive site to the metal detector user. Until the eighteenth century mile trees were used, before being replaced in 1720 by milestones. These trees (which are sometimes marked on maps or once stood in the same position as the milestone stands today) were often used as a congregational point for our ancestors and were the subject of the ancient tradition of 'beating the bounds'.

It is by no means difficult to ascertain the sites of old trees which involve some ritual or hold particular significance, for the majority still stand. Yew trees have occasionally been known to live for three thousand years; they were first introduced to Britain by the Romans. Chestnuts and oaks can live to a tremendous age and because of their permanence were quite frequently chosen as 'marker' trees.

The oak tree claims to be the concealer of most significant finds. Hoards have been found hidden in their hollow trunks, perhaps the proceeds of a robbery or a highwayman's loot. In history, the oak is said to have been the hiding-place of members of royalty, highwaymen and toll collectors. Genuine 'Turpin's oaks' exist around the country and one can only wonder at the number of oaks which concealed highwaymen of lesser fame.

Many of the coach routes of bygone days are usually narrow footpaths today. When using a metal detector along a suspected coach route, remember to search a wider area than the existing path because the original road would have been wide enough for two carts to pass. These old highways may be discovered through research or, as a general guide, by noticing those paths which run in fairly straight lines with ditches either side. Highways such as these are invariably productive to the metal-detecting enthusiast, for treasures must invariably have been dropped by the highwayman in his hurried retreat.

Productive sites will also be found at old toll collection

points. Passenger coaches were frequently used along the thoroughfares after the Roman occupation, and the upkeep of roads was the landowner's responsibility. In return, the landowner would collect tolls for his labour, stationing himself by, or often inside, a 'road landmark tree' (usually an oak) and demanding payment before allowing access. In the early eighteenth century, hollowed oaks were used as the first toll gates; the collector could wait, sheltered, inside the oak, with peepholes cut either side to view the travellers and wave them down. Some landowners insisted upon payment from each passenger and, in order to save time, passengers would throw their coins to the toll collector's tree without the coach stopping. The significance here to the treasure hunter interested in old coins is obvious, for the coach routes were usually muddy and many a coin must have been lost in these conditions.

The golden rule in searching footpaths therefore is never miss an oak tree (especially if it is hollow) nor any other tree of age and significance, for although the oak is the richest in its history, many other trees can be equally productive. Elms may also be hollow and offer a hiding place for the hoard owner, thief, smuggler or child. Three elms known as the 'Old Maid' at Rochford near Paglesham are listed in history as being constantly used by smugglers to conceal their contraband, brought by rowing boat up the River Roche. Many smugglers' treasures have been found in yew trees, including an antique duelling pistol which was discovered on the route of a well-known smugglers' path in Essex.

Oak, ash or chestnut trees were used for the 'Hundred Court', an ancient parliamentary meeting. These trees were called tort trees and a clue is provided as to their locations by noticing which areas have 'tort' in their place names. The Tortworth Chestnut was used as a trysting place by King John where beneath its boughs, the signing of the Magna Carta occurred. Again, footpaths which probably exist today would have led to this tree and they should be kept in mind while searching. It should also be remembered that the tree itself can be effectively searched with a metal detector, paying attention to its boughs, trunk and roots. Care must, of course, be taken not to damage the roots or trunk of the tree through thoughtless and harmful digging.

DUMP DIGGING ON PATHWAYS

Clearly, the highways and byways of our country hold most treasures for those who possess a metal detector but, for the dump digger too, lucrative sites are to be discovered. It has been discussed in Chapter 4 that transport by horse and cart was widely used in the disposal of rubbish in former times. The site chosen for this would have been usually a mile or two from the village and, being frequently used, a pathway would still be apparent today. Paths which appear to lead nowhere and travel only a short distance almost definitely end in an early dumping ground. The site may be indicated by nettles, brambles, hawthorn, and elder which grow abundantly on such sites. Chalk and gravel quarries were commonly used. The pits were filled with refuse over the years and covered naturally by vegetation.

11

BUILDINGS AND URBAN AREAS

The first impression is that treasure hunting and town life are an incompatible combination due to the lack of wide open spaces free from housing estates and industrial buildings. But the urban treasure hunter, interested in metal detecting, dump digging, or rockhounding, has as lucrative a home ground for his hobby as the rural treasure hunter. In the case of metal detecting and dump digging, the rule applies that highly populated areas result in highly productive sites, so that the metal detector user can expect a larger amount of coins, etc., and the dump digger can expect a greater number of dumps. The urban rockhound has a disadvantage when searching actually in a town, but nevertheless finds are to be made if the correct sites are chosen.

METAL DETECTING IN URBAN AREAS

Metal detecting in a town is a positive way to increase a coin collection and can rapidly cover the cost of a detector in modern currency. To achieve this one has only to frequent the local gathering places such as parkland, estate greens, recreation grounds, camping sites, public house gardens, etc., where many lost coins will have accumulated. To make a metal detector pay its way in a town, little imagination and research is necessary for it will be discovered that almost any patch of earth will donate coinage as well as other objects. Grass areas

William Wunderlich and his son with a selection of finds from the site of a medieval fairground.

around telephone boxes, car parks, bus stops, market squares and crossroads are also productive sites.

Older treasures, including hoards of coins, also lie hidden in and around our towns. Long before the introduction of metal detectors, gardeners and, more commonly, builders, have in the course of their work discovered treasure. In 1969, for example, a workman on a Colchester building site discovered a lead casket containing a hoard of ten thousand thirteenth-century longcross pennies in beautiful condition, worth up to £50 each. Similar discoveries, too numerous to mention, have been made in this manner, which enables one to realize the immense potential a metal detector offers.

FAIRGROUNDS

To discover the older treasures and delve into the history of a town, research is generally required to ascertain the relevant

A variety of objects discovered on a site in Sussex including a unique cricket commemorative plaque (*centre*)

sites. The discovery of a medieval fairground site in a town is most significant to the treasure hunter. Mr Wunderlich and his son Mark discovered such a site and from it recovered over 1,200 finds, including some silver pennies and an Edward III groat. Silver hammered coins – including silver deniers which was the main currency used at medieval fairs – jewellery, snuff boxes, silver shoe buckles and antique horseshoes are among the items which may be discovered on a fairground. Fairs have always been immensely popular and the amount of money spent and lost on a site over the years is incalculably high. The scene at the fair was one of much merry-making and entertainment lasting many days and often weeks, and everybody in the area would attend. Throughout the duration of the fair, and within a three mile radius of the site, it was granted that all were immune from arrest so that royalty and vagabonds alike could indulge freely in the celebration. This of course encouraged pickpockets, cutpurses and thieves which greatly contributed towards the reputation which the fair was later accorded of debauchery, rioting and immorality amid the bartering, selling, dancing, feasting and wild entertainment.

Although ancient fairgrounds are usually discovered through research, certain natural features or the presence of a dominant landmark suggest the site of an ancient fair. A chalk carving in a hilltop, for instance, was once used to assist travellers in identifying the location. After Christianity was established in Britain, fairs began to be held on or near the church ground where the clergy endeavoured to keep the fairgoers under control. The fairs were then attributed saints' names, which can provide clues when researching place names. The basis of the medieval fair was its royal charter, for the Crown recognized the event as a substantial addition to their revenue through taxation and, as early as the seventh century, certain towns were granted this royal licence and also allowed to have their own coins minted. These chosen towns were called 'burghs', and 'burgh' or 'borough' in the name of a town indicates that a fair was once held there.

When seeking an ancient fairground one should not dismiss the possibility that a town's existing fairground and circus site may be the same area as that used hundreds of years ago. Even if suspicions are proved wrong and the fairground is only modern, a highly lucrative site will still have been discovered. It is not uncommon for a day's treasure-hunting proceeds to exceed £10 in decimal coinage the day after the fair departs, not to mention all the other valuables which are lost during the fun of the fair. An early start is imperative in reaping the rewards when the fair leaves town, as competition will soon be apparent; even some of the fair stall owners have recognized the potential and can be seen making hurried searches of the area with their detectors before moving to the next town. It is advisable to observe the fair in action and draw a map of all the most productive spots, such as payment points, admission fee areas, roll-a-penny stalls and so on, in preparation for a 'wheel of fortune' all of one's own.

Metal detecting near old gates or thoroughfares should yield a wealth of ornaments and coinage accidentally dropped over the centuries.

Using a metal detector on the site of an old building can reveal the most unlikely objects.

HUNTING IN HOUSES

For the treasure hunter with a metal detector, the dump digger, and in fact for anyone who is interested in recovering some old, and often valuable artefacts, an absorbing pastime is to be found in searching old houses and their grounds. The treasures which have been discovered in old buildings are extensive and extremely valuable. Previous inhabitants may have secreted things in times of invasion or unrest, or merely hidden them because of the lack of banks and as a precaution against thieves.

Long before people began to hunt for these treasures, discoveries were commonly being made by individuals such as builders and new owners of the house who stumbled upon them by chance or accident. In the 1940s an electrician in Wandsworth, London, discovered, under the floorboards of a house, 1,395 bank notes, six gold watches, jewellery and some eighty-four sovereigns and thirty-three half-sovereigns. Beneath a brick fireplace in Over, Cambridge, a teacup full of seventy-eight sovereigns and half-sovereigns was discovered, and in St Osyth, Essex, a barn loft revealed old tea-chests stacked with Georgian silverware. Coin hoards and family wealth continue to be discovered in old houses, especially with the recent interest in treasure hunting as a hobby. In 1977 a couple who were renovating their newly-bought cottage discovered ninety-nine gold sovereigns beneath their floorboards. Treasure hunters who apply their attention to such sites have recovered a vast number of treasures ranging from coin hoards to antique firearms, stamp collections, valuable paintings, odd items of jewellery and even old bottle hoards, such as the one which was recently discovered, worth several hundred pounds, in a cavity of a house in Sussex.

If a house is over fifty years old, it most certainly justifies a search, for within that period ten, perhaps twenty, different families could have occupied the premises, each in turn inevitably forgetting, losing or hiding valuables, and one or

The early twentieth-century elephant knocker and lion's head knocker were found in the grounds of two Kentish houses.

two quite possibly falling victim to some tragedy, never to divulge the secret place of their wealth.

A metal detector, although not essential, may be used to search houses, but slightly different techniques of operation are necessary. A method of 'process elimination' must be employed, i.e. distinguishing the tones emitted by water and gas pipes or the rhythmic signals caused by a line of nails, from the odd signal produced by an unexplained metal object. The detector may be used to search the brickwork of walls or chimney breasts and the woodwork of floors, attic beams and rafters.

The search should commence in the attic, where a variety of treasures could reside. Stamp albums, old books, comics, cigarette cards and the old 78 r.p.m. records, are amongst the more common valuables which occur. Cumbersome old furniture, banished to the loft, may command a high price from a dealer today. Do, however, check all objects before selling them. Many an antique dealer has had a surprise thrown into the bargain when buying old furniture. A bureau in Manchester, for instance, contained secret drawer compartments containing valuable documents and £500 worth of bonds. A loft in London produced another bureau concealing a bag of diamonds worth £3,000!

For searching the rest of the house, a piece of wire is needed, hooked at one end, to retrieve lost coins from beneath skirting boards. Particular attention should be paid to places where the floorboards have sagged to expose a gap as these will prove to be ideal for coins which fall unnoticed from the owner's pocket, coming to rest by the wall until unknowingly kicked beneath the skirting board. The kitchen also deserves special attention beneath skirting boards, as the frequent action of a mop must surely have sent many a coin to rest there. The wire should also be used to check behind mantelpieces which have worked loose from the wall; likewise window-sills, behind pipes, kickboards on doors and crevices between doors and doorsteps. One should consider throughout the search where the owner may have secreted his wealth, where children would have poked the odd coin or trinket into crevices and gaps, and where any other treasure may have been lost. A search should be made of chimney breasts, fireplaces (particularly the ornate type which occasionally have false backs), wall cupboards, staircases, and any cavities which might have been created during renovation of the house.

A search which is made of an inhabited house will no doubt prove a little restricting and, for this reason, many treasure hunters prefer to search derelict houses or houses marked for demolition. As always, the owner of a derelict house must be consulted before work commences and in the case of demolition sites, contractors should also be approached. Demolition contractors are usually only interested in items which have an immediate cash value such as metal fittings, cast iron gutters and railings, lead pipes, etc., and should therefore have little objection to the treasure hunter's interest.

The gardens of houses, particularly if they are old, make an interesting and often very rewarding site. An astounding number of valuable discoveries have been reported over the years by gardeners, who have been well rewarded by the soil for their efforts. In Elland, Yorkshire, in 1932, 1,807 silver coins were found in a jar, buried in the cabbage patch. In a potato patch in Selsey a jar containing 1,000 Roman coins was found by another successful gardener. Perhaps one of the better-known discoveries is that of the golden guineas discovered in Lincolnshire in 1901. After spotting one piece lying on the surface of a flower garden, a search revealed forty more and, by the time word had spread through the village, hundreds more were recovered. Many residents in former times chose, for various reasons, to secrete their wealth close at hand, in their back garden. Although the possibility of finding such treasures are forever present, most metal detector users are quite content to discover the odd coin, children's jewellery and other small items which are common garden finds. It should be remembered, however, that the most productive area of gardens has proved to be around the back doorstep of the house, where a great deal of money would have changed hands when door to door tradesmen were frequent.

DUMP DIGGING IN URBAN AREAS

The dump digger usually has an abundance of lucrative and, usually, more ancient sites in urban areas. Not until the nineteenth century did rubbish disposal become an organized affair, when authorities endeavoured to restrict refuse sites in the towns and cities. In London, for example, areas along the Thames were allocated as dumping sites in the thirteenth century and rubbish was regularly distributed to these points by horse and cart. As the years passed, the problem and build-up of rubbish continued, causing unsightly intrusions upon the streets and encouraging disease in the inhabitants. The people of London took to disposing of their rubbish wherever

Searching an old fireplace for objects hidden behind the brickwork.

Ensure that the structure of a partly dismantled house is sound before commencing a search.

Old railway stations provide an inexhaustible hunting ground for treasure hunters, particularly for those interested in collecting relics of the early railways.

they could, particularly in the tributaries of the Thames until, in 1357, Edward III forbade the practice which was creating an intense problem of pollution. A large quantity of refuse was then sent to brickmakers, who extracted the ashes to blend with clay and make bricks and then dumped the unusable material close to their premises. This practice was widely used and continued into the nineteenth century until the Public Health Act of 1875 was enforced and the responsibility of refuse disposal fell upon local council authorities.

Smaller dumps in urban areas may also be discovered in the gardens of houses dating back to the Victorian era. The house muck hole, which was used until the contents were collected and transported elsewhere, was set up in the garden in an area least conspicuous to the resident; the furthermost point of the garden was usual. The household dump is most commonly recognized by the growth of nettles and an uneven, probably raised, surface. These small household dumps are surprisingly productive, often containing early bottles and pot lids which have been pressed deep into the soil by continual deposit of rubbish. Neither is it uncommon to find the odd engagement or wedding ring which probably fell unnoticed from the kitchen sink and was discarded with the vegetable peelings. Cutlery, old children's toys and other household equipment may well be discovered.

ROCKHOUNDING IN URBAN AREAS

Even the urban rockhound does not have to travel far to enjoy his hobby. Few towns are very far from a constant supply of freshwater, but for those who live in towns which do not have an accessible waterway, it is encouraging to learn that some valuable specimens have in the past been collected from gravel pits, driveways, gardens and parks. Even in the heart of London, jasper and agate are common garden finds. From Charlton Pit near Woolwich, various quartz crystals, including amethyst, may be found along with jasper and cornelian. Wherever there is the will and enthusiasm, rockhounding and other treasurehunting sites abound for urban and rural inhabitants alike.

12
IN THE COUNTRY

Rural treasure hunting has the advantage that its heritage of treasures is more easily accessible than in urban areas. While the prospector and rockhound are in their element in rural areas, it is true to say that for the metal detector user and dump digger, careful research to discover the correct sites is essential before success is achieved. Once this research has been completed, and the more productive sites discovered, the metal detector user certainly benefits from a higher recovery rate of ancient valuables than his urban relative.

SEARCHING FARMLAND
The majority of coin hoards, and many other varied and valuable treasures, have been discovered on farmland with the aid of metal detectors: 2,932 Roman coins (follies) discovered in a Lincolnshire cornfield by the Harrison family; Mr Mayes' find in Norfolk of a large bronze cauldron containing seven other bronze receptacles (all of which were Roman and dated *c.* AD 350), and 201 Roman and Celtic coins found by Bill Parkinson, are a few of the significant finds which would have not been made but for the use of metal detectors. It is not surprising, therefore, that the majority of professional and experienced treasure hunters prefer this type of site to any other and often choose to specialize solely in hunting over wide expanses of farmland.

A bronze cauldron and other utensils dating from the Roman occupation found in a field in Norfolk.

Roman and Anglo-Saxon artefacts discovered on Kentish farmland with a metal detector.

Anglo-Saxon cloak clasps found in a ploughfield.

The advantage of searching farmland is that it is inexhaustible of treasures, for the same piece of land may be searched time and time again and still produce results. The percolating effect which the earth has on objects buried in the soil is expedited by the working of soil on farmland, especially by the action of a plough. With its vast range of prospects and inexhaustible stock of finds, little more could be asked by any treasure hunter.

SEARCHING FRUIT-PICKING FIELDS

Fruit-picking fields, which employ casual labour, are lucrative sites to search. Let us consider the potential of the hop-picking fields alone, which is an ideal site to encourage both the novice and professional metal detector user.

Hop plantations first came into being as early as 1552 and by 1920 some fifty thousand acres were involved, thirty thousand of which were in Kent. In the late nineteenth century, there was a large boom in the hop industry which was to last many years. Men, women and children of all ages, particularly from London, would descend upon the hop fields to pick the produce. Thousands of people would spend their summer months in this way, which served as a happy, healthy and profitable holiday.

Throughout the daylight hours a good deal of money was continually changing hands and inevitably being lost. The sweet van and ice cream seller would visit the site, usually twice a day. The paying out of wages was conducted each working day. The accidental losses on a hop-picking site were incalculably high for, as any hop-picker knows, hardly a day passes without at least one person losing a ring or other item of value.

Hopping tokens earned by the hop-pickers are a find which one may well come across. These tokens were first produced in the mid eighteenth century and were widely used throughout the boom of the hop industry. Each hop grower would design a token of his own and would often compete with others to produce the most attractive. The tokens represented the number of bushels picked and could later be cashed for money or goods by the picker. Lead was the most common material used by the producer, but brass and copper tokens also existed.

SOCIAL SITES AND DUMPS

The rural metal detector user may also find rewarding sites by researching into the locations of harvest festivals, fairgrounds, favourite Victorian picnic areas and other areas where social activity would, in the past, have taken place. For those who are interested in modern valuables, such as decimal currency, much will be gleaned from searching camping grounds when the summer season is over and holiday-makers have departed.

Hop pickers' huts can still be located in the hop fields of Kent and Sussex. Although the huts themselves may be relatively recent, it is probable that a series of temporary shelters has been on that site for many years.

Dump digging as a hobby has now become more popular in rural areas as many of the major dumps of the towns and cities are being exhausted. Garden and village dumps are never far from places of habitation. It is quite common to discover three or four dumps which served a small community. Research into old parish records will provide yet more sites, including areas where town and city refuse was distributed in the countryside. Dumps situated near brickworks may also be discovered through research. The dumps which are to be found around these, often derelict, buildings are vast for they were once a major outlet for the problem of city refuse. The location of the material which was dumped is never far from the site of the brickworks and often takes the form of a large mound extending across a considerable area of land. Depending on how important the brickworks was in its time, a number of dumps may exist. Nettles, brambles or pieces of glass and pottery usually mark the site.

ROCKHOUNDING AND PROSPECTING IN RURAL AREAS

Rockhounding and prospecting for gold are best achieved in rural areas as will be seen even from the most casual glance at a geological map. Igneous rock (usually marked in red) is favourable for rockhounding. Rivers in igneous areas have already been discussed as lucrative hunting grounds, but quarries, gravel pits and disused mines are popular with the rockhound and prospector. Gravel pits are most common in lowland Britain, but a considerable number may also be found in the Highlands of Scotland. Gravel deposits came about when the melting ice sheets of the Ice Age conveyed sand and gravel to many areas throughout Britain; they are called fluvio-

A typical derelict brickworks with a dump in front of it.

Silver pennies, a medieval token (*centre*) and thimbles discovered on the ancient site of a Welsh fair.

glacial deposits. These deposits often occur along the course of rivers, such as the River Trent where gravel pits exist in abundance along its banks. Fossils and gemstones are plentiful, particularly quartz, chalcedony and agates. In the gravel pits of the Scottish Highlands, garnets are not difficult to find.

The spoil heaps of mines and quarries are well worth searching by the rockhound and certainly by the prospector if the mine was used to excavate gold. Cornwall is particularly rich in gemstones which may be obtained from the old tin and copper mines where, in the spoil heaps, turquoise has been found. Cornish china-clay pits offer an abundance of quartz from their white heaps, usually amethyst, smoky quartz, rock crystal and citrine (lemon-coloured quartz). Specimens of turquoise and black tourmaline, beryl, apatite, fluorspar, serpentine, tin and copper minerals, even silver ores, can be found among the wide variety of other rocks and minerals in the Cornish spoil heaps. Scotland has similarly productive mining sites, including the old gold mining areas which still provide specimens of this precious mineral for the prospector.

13

INCREASING THE YIELD

It cannot be denied that treasures at times possess an uncanny knack of turning up in the most unexpected locations. A prime example is that of a grave which was excavated by a group of archaeologists where, many years ago, a thief had been hanged and buried for his misdeeds. The group were greatly astonished when, from the thief's armpit, fell one of the best specimens of a William the Conqueror penny ever found.

This is of course one of the exceptions. Successful treasure hunting is generally the direct result of diligent and dedicated research. The satisfaction of substantiating perhaps a mere hunch leading to long research before the discovery of treasure is incomparable to a discovery which was the result of a chance find. The difference may be likened to the inheritance of wealth as opposed to the fulfilment which one must feel when rewards are the result of one's own efforts. Research to the treasure hunter not only dramatically increases yield, but also provides a most enjoyable and educational task which contributes half of the ingredients for the hobby's enjoyment and success.

Few treasure hunters, in particular metal detector users, dedicate their attention towards research and not surprisingly, the majority fall by the wayside, disappointed with results and bewildered by the task of choosing a site. The rockhound cannot expect to achieve a collection unless he is competent in his knowledge of identification and rock formation. Similarly, the prospector must have some knowledge of identification, the circumstances in which gold occurs and research into the sites where gold has in the past been recovered. For the beachcomber, metal detector user and dump digger, research has to extend further than reading literature directly related to the subject and may involve long hours of poring over books and records in pursuit of a vital literary trail before the actual search may commence. The problem which many treasure hunters face, however, is one of knowing just where to look for a lead to follow when seeking a productive site. The following pages list just a few of the sources which deserve attention, all of which are available to the public in local archives and libraries.

OLD NEWSPAPERS

Old newspapers provide an abundance of relevant information to the treasure hunter and may be found in libraries, where the major local or county paper is retained for twenty years, or from the County Record Office where newspapers usually date back to the 1800s. Regardless of the type of site one wishes to specialize in, or the nature of the treasure hunting activity in which one's interest is centred, clues and information may be found. An 1817 newspaper, for instance, read thus:

A canal boat containing 170 persons on a holiday excursion to Birmingham sank on Easter Monday in a canal at Smethwick, in six and a half feet of water. Everyone escaped miraculously.

No mention was made as to their possessions. Similarly, for the metal detector user whose interest lies in recovering items from the Canal Age, a news item such as the one in a Scottish local paper of 1887 would be of interest. It reported a notice which had just been erected by the Crinan Canal Company and read:

Children and Others are hereby prohibited from running along the

Canal Banks after the Passenger Steamer; and Passengers are requested not to encourage them by throwing money onto the bank. Children are further warned not to throw flowers into the boat.

The stories of treasure hoard recoveries would have appeared in newspapers of the past and this also holds special significance to the treasure hunter, for before metal detectors existed, it is certain that at least one item of the hoard would have escaped recovery. Even a report of only one ancient coin being recovered could mean that this was part of a scattered hoard and certainly deserves further research.

Other news items such as robberies, fires, floods, battles, etc., all merit consideration. Lost and found columns of old newspapers are give-away sites to the metal detector user, though the owner, if still obtainable, should be informed if the item is recovered.

Dump sites can also be discovered through reading past news, for the problem of refuse disposal has been of public concern for centuries. The sites utilized for this purpose would be publicly announced in the local newspaper and its whereabouts described in detail. A number of the sites may well be obliterated beneath housing developments but this should not necessarily deter the dump digger from his discovery. A friendly approach to one of the residents may reveal that he is willing to allow a search of his vegetable patch in return for the earth being worked in readiness for his next year's produce.

MAPS

Maps are an essential piece of equipment from which many lucrative sites can be discovered. The rockhound and prospector should study geological maps to discover the productivity of areas according to the rock types which occur. The beachcomber should acquire a chart of the sea in order to gain a better understanding of the coast on which he is working, and the metal detector user and dump digger require

An old map shows the site of a racecourse unmarked by physical features today.

The original Pilgrims Way, a footpath, is to the right of the obvious track, which was probably developed to take large carts and coaches.

maps both ancient and modern to understand and compare the possibilities of the land.

Sea charts are easily obtainable and offer a great deal of information to the beachcomber, although they are primarily produced to assist seamen in navigation. These charts not only list features of the sea but also display the surrounding land, illustrating landmarks such as churches, castles, towers, etc., for the benefit of seamen who may take their bearings from the sightings of such points. By studying the actual coastline the beachcomber may observe potentially lucrative spots such as restricted harbour mouths where harsher wave activity and greater erosion generally constitute favourable beachcombing ground. The sites of wrecks are also marked on a sea chart and it is possible for the beachcomber to consider the approximate destination point of items which may be freed in the event of stormy seas, according to currents which are apparent.

A most enjoyable task for the metal detector user and dump digger is discovered by comparing old maps with new and, if done in the correct manner, a profitable exercise is also the result. Hundred-year-old Ordnance Survey maps and modern Ordnance Survey maps of local areas are both to be found in the reference sections of local libraries. Although these are quite adequate for the purpose required, reproductions of older maps may also be obtained from bookshops and publishers. Assuming that a hundred-year-old and a modern Ordnance Survey map have been chosen of an area, an indication is given below of the type of information which may be extracted.

The dump digger should use the ancient map to determine such sites as brickworks, clay and chalk pits, and footpaths which lead to no significant destination and thus suggest a dumping ground at its end. It was mentioned in Chapter 9 that river embankments constructed in the Victorian era were comprised largely of household rubbish. The dump digger should study and compare the course of a river on the two

Two stones signifying places of ancient ritual or superstition where coins may have been dropped. The stones themselves are protected under the Historic Monuments Act but, with permission, the surrounding areas can be searched.'

maps and it will be found that discrepancies occur in a few places. This could be due to natural causes, but in many cases the reason is that an embankment was built to alter the water's course. Artificial river embankments are sometimes marked on maps by a series of short black lines.

Comparing the course of a river also holds significance to the metal detector user, for it may be discovered that such points as fords or bridges were once in different positions. Extinct features along the river's banks may be discovered, such as ferries, watermills, and riverside public houses.

In a similar manner, the course of footpaths should be compared. The photograph of the existing Pilgrims Way shows the deceptive placing of the signpost with regard to the small ancient track which runs parallel only a few feet to its right. This can be a common occurrence in the case of footpaths, for when the original track became worn down and muddy people chose to walk beside the path, especially if it was on higher ground, until eventually a new path was formed.

PARISH RECORDS AND COUNCIL MINUTES

Parish records and Council minutes are another source quite often overlooked by the metal detector user and dump digger when delving into local history. Parish records date back often to the early seventeenth century and, as with Council minutes, can be found in the reference section of libraries. Council minutes will certainly refer to refuse sites, as it was the Council's responsibility to supervise them, and many other useful pieces of information regarding public amenities will be found of relevance to the metal detector user. Parish records provide an in-depth guide to the former way of life in a parish and the metal detector user may be able to extract the locations of such functions as fairs, tea parties, Sunday school excursions, picnic areas, village fêtes, playgrounds and so on.

DIRECT CONVERSATION

Talking to local residents of an area one plans to search is often one of the most fruitful methods of research. The older folk of a community are usually only too happy to reminisce about the way life used to be, and this to the dump digger, beachcomber and metal detector user is of great importance. Elderly locals will usually be able to inform the dump digger of the whereabouts of the old dump where, as children, they would most probably have collected the glass stoppers from Codd bottles to use as marbles, once a common practice. The beachcomber may also benefit from local inhabitants' knowledge in discovering the sites of former attractions such as Punch and Judy shows and refreshment stalls, or the whereabouts of smugglers' paths and shipwrecks. Sites no longer marked by landscape features can be searched with a metal detector, ranging from an old ferry site on a river to the site of a medieval fairground, or suspected treasure hoard.

FOLKLORE

Folk tales are common in most areas and many will be concerned with treasure in various forms. Verbally handed down from generation to generation, such tales are inevitably misconstrued and often exaggerated through the years, rendering the modern version difficult both to decipher and to believe. Nevertheless, there will probably be a basis of fact which will provide the treasure hunter with a fascinating and worthwhile project to follow. Often described in folklore are tales of treasures guarded by demons, curses or other supernatural entities and it is highly probable that these tales were deliberately constructed to deter inquisitive souls from seeking the wealth. A typical example is the tale of Rillaton Barrow which was told thus:

On Bodmin Moor, Cornwall, people used to warn travellers of a Druid priest who sat motionless in a chair-shaped rock, extending one arm which enticingly offered a golden cup containing a magic potion to passers-by. It was told that one victim, a drunken hunter who took no heed of the local folks' warnings, met the Druid and, instead of refusing his potion, accepted eagerly. He threw the potion into the Druid's face and galloped off laughing furiously and grasping the golden chalice triumphantly in his hand. Soon after this, three villagers found the horse and rider dead. Terrified to even touch the golden chalice which the hunter still clutched, the villagers buried him and the chalice together in what later became known as Rillaton Barrow.

For many years the locals told this tale about the barrow. In 1818, it was excavated and found to contain a skeleton and a golden beaker.

Superstitions and primitive beliefs are also worthy of investigation by the treasure hunter, especially those of local origin which may again be discovered through talking to residents or studying local folklore. In Yorkshire, dairymaids would leave a crooked silver sixpence on a 'witchpost' to effect what they called a 'churn spell' to ensure good butter. The been taken by witches so another would be put in its place. In Wales, brass amulets were buried near stables in the belief that this would deter witches from stealing the horses at night and riding them until exhausted before manipulating their characters to become untrustworthy and vicious. The brass amulets, usually in the shape of a sun, crescent or wheel, were later worn on the horse's bridle and from this evolved the practice of decorating horses with brasses. Another primitive belief stipulated that plants or trees needed some kind of sacrifice before they would oblige by growing. In the parish of Scotton in Lincolnshire, a number of ash trees were felled in 1880 and under each was discovered a horseshoe. In Suffolk a farmer recently found that when walnut trees were felled on his land, a gold coin was found beneath each one.

ANCIENT CUSTOMS

The treasure hunter with a metal detector also benefits from looking into ancient traditions, customs and ceremonies to discover their locations and realize the potential they offer. In a time when much dependence was placed upon the productivity of a farm, ceremonies and celebrations were common to encourage fertility. These were in fact the very beginning of the ancient fair, and were usually held at the time of the solstices to welcome in the new season. However, it is usually difficult to discover the site on which these early celebrations were held. For this reason it is important that the treasure hunter should study the layout of the land to understand the significance that certain features once held.

Although an entire book could be devoted to the ancient customs which surround natural landscape features, below are a few explaining the importance of significant stones which have relevance to the treasure hunter with a metal detector. The finds connected with stones are usually buried and widely scattered around the site.

Stones were often used as boundaries between two parishes and were a point at which various ceremonies took place, such as beating the bounds, whipping and often worship. Although few of these stones now exist in the original position due to the Christian Church's disapproval of their influence on the parish, books concerning folklore, old maps and parish records will provide clues as to their former locations. Stones of this kind, often taking the shape of large boulders, would have been frequently visited in the past by our ancestors, as objects involving superstitions and early customs. Some were worshipped for general good luck, others for fertility, health, wealth and prosperity, and so on. The Church's order for their removal was no easy task, and for many stones impossible, as removal usually involved a team of horses, chains and reluctant men who feared the fate which might befall them.

Healing stones most commonly took the form of large

standing boulders with natural or carved holes in them. They were used particularly for the cure of children's illnesses, whereby the affected child would be passed three times through the hole and an offering would be left or a coin would be thrown high into the air. A typical example of such a stone is the Men-an-Tol in Cornwall. Another example is that of St Declan's stone in County Waterford where thousands of pilgrims used to go to seek a cure for rheumatic ailments. Loch Manor in the Scottish Highlands is said to contain stones with healing properties and pilgrims would enter the water at midnight and throw a coin.

Plague stones were used in virtually every town throughout Britain at the time of the plague. These stones had indentations which were filled with vinegar. Farmers would leave provisions beside the stone and, in return, the townsfolk would place money in the vinegar. A great number of these stones are still undiscovered but some of the better known ones include the Pest Basin in the churchyard of St Giles at Shrewsbury and the Merival Row, a number of stones on Dartmoor which were used when the plague spread to Tavistock in 1625.

Stones with hollowed summits were used as payment points in former times. Sometimes they can be recognized as tythe stones where for centuries farmers would place their tithes for collection by the lord of the manor.

KEEPING RECORDS

Record keeping is invariably a method used by the most successful of treasure hunters which surely proves its worth. For the general treasure hunter this should consist of research notes, a finds record and, for the metal detector user, a scrapbook.

Research notes soon accumulate over the months and should be kept continually up-to-date. The collected information will be found to piece together like a jigsaw in many cases and will

Carry your research notes with you when working on a site so that observations can be jotted down systematically.

The correctly labelled finds made during a one-day outing by the Bournemouth and District Metal Detecting Club.

result in a better knowledge of local history. It will also be discovered that research into one site usually provides information leading to the discovery of another potential site.

Recording finds is beneficial to the beachcomber, dump digger, rockhound, metal detector user and prospector alike, for it is found in each case that where one treasure is discovered, more are highly likely to occur. The record would include the name of the site visited, the type of find and its age (where applicable). This has a number of advantages to the treasure hunter and also to any authority or interested person who required information regarding a discovery.

Keeping a scrap-book is a method of increasing yield which surprisingly few metal detector users consider. Newspaper cuttings and other informative notes regarding valuables which have been discovered in a locality should all be entered in this book. Discoveries such as old coins found by gardeners or metal detector users are of interest and over a period of time study of the book may reveal that a particular type of coin has turned up on different occasions in close proximity which, to the optimistic treasure hunter, could well mean the presence of a hoard.

14

COLLECTING AND CLEANING

The enjoyment of discovering a rare coin, bottle, mineral or other valuable item, often begins when the finder has returned home where he can clean and identify his find before giving it a place in his collection. From the time the treasure hunter slips such muddy or sand-encrusted items into his pocket to the time they have undergone cleaning and restoration, incredible transformations can occur. A ring possessed for many years by the sea might appear irretrievably corroded or insignificant until it has been cleaned correctly to restore it to its full beauty. Bottles, pot lids and pipes offer similar surprises and even if incomplete, ceramics can be restored and pieced back together almost perfectly. Dull pebbles which the rockhound has collected can be polished into beautiful gems fit for the finest of jewellery or an attractive display at the least.

Presentation of a collection inspires pride and incentive not only for the collector, but also for others who are interested in such pursuits. But there is much to be learnt in the art of restoration; mistakes are irreversible and, all too often, disastrous for the subjected item. 'Rare, but has been cleaned' is a description frequently seen in coin catalogues at auctions and demonstrates how cleaning some coins can automatically decrease their value drastically. The same can be true of bottles, jewellery and valuables of virtually any other description, if they are over-cleaned or if the wrong cleaning methods are used. Cleaning techniques and restoration methods should therefore be fully understood by the collector and undertaken according to the find's age and condition, rarity and value, material and type. Whenever there is any doubt about these factors or in identification of the object, the golden rule in restoration is, *don't*. Take the item and obtain expert advice from a museum or other specialist.

All the chemicals mentioned below are available in stock or by order from chemists' shops; artists' suppliers and hardware shops can usually supply crocus powder, epoxy resin, jewellers' rouge and whiting. It cannot be over-emphasized that great care should be taken when working with chemicals. Safety glasses should be worn when using acid solutions and good ventilation is essential to disperse fumes. Never leave chemicals within reach of children.

Bearing these points in mind, we may now look at some of the methods used, commencing with the restoration of metals.

RESTORING GOLD
Gold is an inert metal and is therefore unaffected by corrosive elements. Even the destructiveness of the sea does not corrode or discolour the brilliance of pure gold, and if the item has deteriorated this is a sure sign that the object is not pure. Purity of gold is expressed in carats: the scale ranges from twenty-four carats, which is the purest but also the softest, to nine carats, which is the hardest but of least value for it is mixed with fifteen parts of hardening metal. The deterioration of gold relates according to its carat value, so that high purity gold will need no more than a wash in soapy water and a polish with a soft cloth to restore its beauty. Tarnish on low carat gold may be removed by cleaning in a ten per cent ammonia solution, and blemishes can be treated with jewellers' rouge.

RESTORING SILVER
Silver corrodes and tarnishes rapidly when exposed to the

An embossed copper strip prior to cleaning by electrolysis.

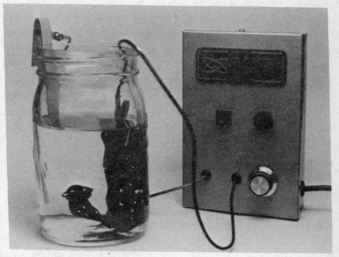

The 'coin cleaner' in action.

The copper strip after cleaning. The rivet holes and decoration are now clearly revealed.

elements of the soil and, especially, the sea. Black discolouring is the characteristic of tarnished silver and is known as 'patina'. The best method of cleaning silver is with a silver dip, which may be made by lining a bowl with aluminium foil and filling it with a solution of one pint of hot water and a third of a cup of washing soda. The silver can then be placed in the solution, but must be carefully watched. Electrochemical activity can be seen to occur by small bubbles coming off the object. As soon as the tarnish has been removed, it must be taken from the solution and thoroughly rinsed in hot water, for too much dipping leaves the object with a pallid appearance. A ten per cent ammonia solution assists in removing corrosion, and crocus powder may be used to polish.

It should be remembered, however, that silver often acquires a bluish-green tint which is often referred to as 'tone'. This enhances the value of the item and should not be removed.

RESTORING COPPER

Copper often acquires a powdery green surface called 'verdigris'. This must never be confused with patina which is brown or green and discolours evenly. Patina is formed through a chemical reaction between the metal's surface and the atmosphere; it protects the item from destructive elements and also enhances the value. Verdigris should be removed by softening with a light oil (such as vegetable oil) and, if the condition of the object permits, encrustation may be removed from crevices after softening with a wooden cocktail stick, the end of which should be soaked in water to make it pliable.

A solution of washing soda will remove most corrosion, but when more drastic methods are needed for copper, the item should be immersed in a hot ten per cent potassium oxatate or hydrochloric acid solution. A constant watch should be made of the progress and when the desired effect is achieved, thorough washing and rinsing must follow to prevent damage to the surface.

RESTORING BRONZE

Bronze discolours in a similar way to copper and often has patina which must never be removed. Verdigris can be removed with vegetable oil as with copper and the washing soda solution given on page 166 should remove much of the corrosion. It is useful to remember also that unpleasant stains may be removed without destroying patina by careful application of half a lemon dipped in salt.

RESTORING BRASS

Brass, according to the type of object, may be cleaned with modern household brass cleaners. An equally effective solution may be made by mixing spirit of turpentine with whiting to make a smooth paste. When more drastic cleaning is necessary, deep tarnish can be removed with a ten per cent oxalic acid solution applied with a rag, followed by thorough washing and drying with whiting.

RESTORING CAST IRON

Cast iron objects may at first seem undesirable material for the treasure hunter to collect, but some ornate and beautiful pieces are often discovered and can date back to 300 BC. Unfortunately, cast iron rusts considerably and the first step in its preservation is to remove this with a wire brush and paint it with a rust proofer. For the purpose of a collection, or if the item is not of extreme age or value, matt black paint can be used to display it at its best.

CLEANING COINS

The above methods may also be used to clean coins, which should then be preserved and protected by enclosing them in plastic coin envelopes.

Another method used to clean coins and items with intricate designs is that of electrolysis which enables access to all the small crevices of the item. Although numismatists are still wary of its use on valuable coins, the 'coin cleaner' (as it is popularly known) is capable of removing substantial corrosion on all types of metals provided the correct techniques are employed.

The apparatus is readily available from treasure hunting shops at a reasonable price. The electrolysis method, very briefly involves the passing of a direct current between the item to be cleaned and another metal object, both of which are immersed in a conducting solution. The electricity breaks up the chemical compound surrounding the item and causes gases to be liberated between each electrode which can be seen in the form of tiny bubbles. The voltage and solution varies according to the item to be cleaned, but basically an acid solution is used, commonly consisting of half a teaspoon of salt, one teaspoon of citric acid and one and a half pints of warm water. The item to be cleaned serves as one electrode and the other is usually a one-inch strip of stainless steel. Both electrodes are suspended by crocodile clips leading from the coin cleaner into a glass container where they are placed in the prepared solution. When the two electrodes are arranged so that they are opposite each other, the cleaner may be switched on. Never allow the two electrodes to touch while the cleaner is switched on.

Constant supervision should be maintained throughout the process, so that as soon as the corrosion is gone, the item may be removed and washed immediately. It is also important that the solution is changed and the apparatus thoroughly cleaned after use with each metal type, i.e. all silver may be cleaned in one solution, but it must be changed before cleaning copper. Unless this rule is observed, it will be found that more harm is done in the process than good; silver cleaned in a solution which has contained copper will turn red.

Spendable coinage which has been collected by the beach-comber and metal detector user, will be found to have corroded drastically, especially if found on a beach. A cleaning process is therefore necessary which involves little time and effort to render it fit for exchange. A solution of half a pint of white vinegar mixed with three tablespoons of cooking salt produces the desired effect. The solution must be changed when cleaning coins of different metals, and each coin requires rinsing in fresh water when the corrosion has been removed. Modern currency may be cleaned by placing it in a container of two tablespoons of salt diluted in one pint of water and adding a handful of crushed milk bottle tops. A few hours of this process removes the majority of corrosion, the remainder of which should then respond to cleaning with a soft toothbrush and washing in fresh water.

CLEANING AND RESTORING DUMP FINDS: BOTTLES

The majority of glassware retrieved from a dump is relatively simple to clean, provided that a few basic rules are observed. It must be remembered that these items have lain undisturbed at fairly constant levels of temperature and pressure for a number of years and that their exposure to the atmosphere and cleaning procedures can have drastic effects upon their condition. To reduce the risk of damage, bottles should be left in the open for a few days to allow them to acclimatize before cleaning commences. Hot water should never be used on glass and it will be discovered that the washing soda and water solution (see page 166) is quite adequate to cleanse the bottles if they are allowed to soak for a week or more. Deposits which remain inside the bottle may be removed with the careful use of a bottle brush and for persistent stains, a solution of equal parts of household bleach and water is usually adequate. Lettering on the outside of a bottle tends to collect grime which should respond to a soft toothbrush or wooden cocktail stick.

'Sickness' is a term used by bottle collectors to describe a white residue which is apparent on the bottle and is caused by chemicals present in the dump. Sickness does however suggest age for it is found mainly on bottles of sixty years old or more.

A white residue is called 'opalescence', and where it reflects rainbow colours it is called 'iridescence' which can look attractive. Although some people prefer to leave sick bottles in the state in which they are found, as a symbol of antiquity, it is a fact that a sick bottle will sell for considerably less at auction. If the bottle is rare, expert advice should be sought, for the only real cure is to treat them with strong acids, unavailable to the public. For display purposes, however, the rough surface of a sick bottle can be polished with a Brillo pad or steel wool and Brasso. To obtain a finish, T-cut liquid abrasive or rouge and crocus powder is used; many collectors apply a coat of polyurethane varnish as a final touch.

Glass may also be renovated and with practice the art can be developed to such a degree that bottles with broken necks, bases or lips can be rendered looking as good as new. This is done with the use of epoxy resin, which may be coloured with pigments (available at artists' suppliers) to match the bottle. The resin is moulded into the appropriate shape and held in place by cellulose tape until dry, then finished with a coat of polyurethane varnish.

CLAY PIPES

The first stage in the cleaning of clay pipes is to wash them in warm soapy water with a soft toothbrush. This will remove surface dirt and enable an inspection of the number and type of stains present. The majority of clay pipes were unglazed and it will therefore be found that stains penetrate deep into the porous material. This requires patient cleaning to remove all marks. Rust stains commonly found on pipes retrieved from dumps can be removed by soaking them in a twenty-five per cent solution of orthophosphoric acid. This can be mixed by your supplier or at home. When the rust has disappeared, rinse the pipes thoroughly in warm water. To remove all traces of the acid, which would otherwise destroy these finds, soak the pipes in fresh water changed daily for three days.

Nicotine stains can be removed by soaking the pipe in household bleach. Again the process of washing and soaking should follow in order to remove the bleach thoroughly.

It was mentioned in Chapter 4 that all pieces of broken stems or bowls should be collected, for they are of great assistance in the renovation fo incomplete specimens. A pipe with a broken stem may be renovated by choosing another stem of equal diameter and joining the two together. The stem should be cut to the correct length and the joining ends filed smooth before glueing them with epoxy resin. The adhesive will require a dye to match the pipe's colour and this is mixed before being applied. To renovate broken bowls, experts use Cascamite powdered resin glue dyed to the correct colour, which may be used as a filler to replace missing sections of bowl. Dyes commonly used are stannic oxide which has a slightly cream-coloured effect or titanium dioxide for white.

POT LIDS

Because of their glaze, pot lids are usually found in presentable condition after the surface dirt has been attended to, and a wash in soapy water is quite adequate. Obstinate stains often respond to the use of household bleach, following the same instructions as for clay pipes, of long soaking and rinsing to eliminate the risk of bleach remaining in the article – it may seep through cracks in the glaze. Abrasive cleaners should never be used on glazed ceramics, for the item will be instantly devalued by collectors if cleaning is obvious.

Cascamite waterproof putty may be used to fill in broken rims or repair chips. The mixture should be applied generously, allowed to dry, then rubbed down to the correct shape.

POLISHING PEBBLES

This final stage of rockhounding is popularly the most

enjoyable and rewarding aspect of the hobby. From dull-coloured pebbles beautiful stones with mirror finishes are the end result, suitable for display and jewellery. Patience is the key to success in polishing stones, for although the process does not involve hard work unless polished by hand, a wait of approximately four weeks is usually necessary before the process is complete. Nevertheless, the methods used are quicker and far in advance of the natural method which pebbles undergo by the sea's action, although modern techniques are based on the same principle. In the most popular and effective method of 'tumbling' stones, a mixture of grits with water is used on the pebbles which rotate together inside a drum for a number of days depending on the type of pebble.

Hand polishing is used when rock specimens are too large or small for tumble polishing and is achieved by a mixture of grits and polish used on a plate of glass. The coarse grit is mixed with enough water to make it moist and the stone is rubbed into this, on the plate of glass, in a circular motion until all pitted marks are removed and a smooth surface is obtained. The glass and pebbles are then rinsed thoroughly, until no trace of the former grit is present. The process is repeated with a finer grit and then, finally, the polish. The same grits are used as with the tumbling method, starting with silicon carbide grit 80, then silicon carbide grit 400 and finally cerium or tin oxide to polish.

Tumbling machines work by a small electric motor which turns rollers, thus rotating the drum which is situated on them. Choosing a suitable tumbler depends greatly upon the amount of pebbles one is likely to collect, for this will determine the size and type necessary. A one-and-a-half-pound barrel, for instance, will carry only a hundred small stones, whereas a three-pound barrel will carry two hundred and so on. It should be remembered that the process for one batch will take approximately four weeks and that one hundred pebbles can easily be collected in a few days' rockhounding. A

A twin-barrel tumble polisher is the most satisfying type to use if you are a regular collector of interesting pebbles.

very popular and more ideal tumbler is the 'twin barrel', which enables two separate batches to be processed at the same time. This is particularly advantageous in that hard and soft stones (which must always be kept separate) may be tumbled side by side and therefore reach the finished stage together.

When a suitable tumbling machine has been purchased, the process may then commence, and the first stage is to sort the collected pebbles into soft and hard types for each tumbling process. Soft pebbles would quickly break down and interfere with the process if tumbled with harder pebbles, so the temptation of tumbling them together must be avoided. Agate, chalcedony, quartz, jasper and flint for instance should be tumbled together as harder stones. A selection of sizes, usually ranging from small chips to walnut size, assist in tumbling the stones more efficiently and a few larger stones may be added if the size of the barrel permits. It is worth noting, however, that the stones will decrease to as much as half their size by the time the process has finished, so that very small stones which are of particular interest are perhaps better polished by hand. At this stage, unsuitable pebbles should be rejected, such as very badly pitted specimens, or cracked, porous and flaky pebbles.

The barrel may then be loaded with the pebbles to a capacity of not less than two-thirds and not more than three-quarters full. The coarse grit (silicon carbide grit 80–100) is used first, in quantities depending upon the barrel size. For a one-and-a-half-pound barrel, use one heaped tablespoon of grit, for a three-pound barrel, two heaped tablespoons and so on. Add sufficient water to just cover the stones, firmly replace the lid and commence tumbling. After seven days of continuous tumbling, the stones may be inspected, by taking half a dozen or so and washing them, to study their progress. If the majority still have pit marks, the process should continue longer, adding more water if necessary or grit if it has become too fine. Fourteen days is common for the first stage and it is worth being painstaking to remove all marks; progressing to a finer grit when the stones are not ready will produce inferior results. It is rarely, if ever, possible to remove pits from all the stones at the same time, so when four or five out of six have reached the desired condition, the next stage may then commence. Sub-standard stones should be removed and set aside to tumble again with a future load.

It is imperative that before the second stage proceeds, thorough washing of stones and equipment is undertaken. The stones are poured gently from the barrel into a plastic sieve over an old saucepan or similar container and rinsed thoroughly under fresh water. The grit should never be thrown down the sink, for blockage problems would be almost certain. The barrel must also be well cleaned, so that no particles of the coarser grit remain.

Repeat the same process for the second stage, using the same quantities of the finer grit (silicon carbide grit 400). After six days the stones may be inspected every twenty-four hours although ten days for the second stage is normal. When the pebbles are free of scratches and blemishes, they are ready for the polishing stage, after thorough cleaning has again been administered. The slightest amount of grit contamination in the final stage will completely ruin the mirror finish which should be achieved and for this reason, some prefer to use one barrel of a twin barrel tumbler solely for polishing purposes. Care must also be taken at this stage not to crack the pebbles by allowing them to knock together while cleaning. For this reason, the barrel must be loaded with the correct amount of pebbles, for if there are too few, the risk of their damaging each other is greater.

The third stage of polishing is accomplished in the same manner as previous stages. One teaspoon of cerium or tin oxide is used for every one-and-a-half-pound tumbling capacity and the process usually takes seven days. At the end of this some beautiful and perhaps valuable stones should be the result.

15
THE LEGAL ASPECT

At some time or another, if the treasure hunter is dedicated in his quest, a significant discovery will very probably occur. It is therefore essential that the finder is aware of his rights and his obligations, so that he may act responsibly and legally to reap the rewards of his success. To say the least, it would be a grave disappointment to learn that the find is liable to confiscation because it was acquired illegally or improperly dealt with, and ignorance of such actions is no excuse in the eyes of the law.

Looking on the brighter side, it is a fact that if precautions are taken and discoveries are promptly reported, the old saying of 'finders keepers' usually holds good. Certainly this is the case under the treasure trove laws which merely decide whether the finder can keep his treasure to do with as he will, or whether he shares it with the public by having it displayed in a museum and receives its full market value.

Clearly the treasure hunter cannot lose so long as he has fulfilled all his obligations by acting within the laws which surround his hobby, before and after the event of a significant discovery, unless of course the previous owner can be traced. This aspect will be dealt with subsequently in detail, but consideration must also be paid to aspects which not only concern the detector user, but the beachcomber, dump digger, rockhound and prospector also. Such laws as trespass and neglecting to declare significant discoveries apply to all, and failure to comply with them can result in confiscation of the proceeds, fines and/or imprisonment. It is obvious then, that there is every reason why one should be aware of the legal aspects of treasure hunting before the event of a valuable discovery and not after it has occurred, when it is often too late to rectify one's errors or ignorance.

LICENCES

The initial legal requirement for the metal detector user is that he possess a licence to operate his machine. The reason for this is to ensure that the detector stated in the application performs under the correct specifications so as not to interfere with radio frequencies. The fee for a licence is £1.40 for four years and application forms may be acquired from metal detector manufacturers or direct from the Home Office, Accounts Branch, Tolworth Tower, Ewell Road, Surbiton, Surrey KT6 7DS.

For the metal detector user in Ireland, an additional licence is required to permit a person to search for artefacts. In Northern Ireland this is enforced under the Historic Monuments Act 1971, and south of the border under the terms of the National Monuments Act 1930.

ARCHAEOLOGICAL SITES

It is an offence to hunt for treasure in the grounds of scheduled archaeological sites or on or near ancient monuments. The consequences of plundering such sites are severe fines and/or imprisonment, not to mention the bad reputation it gives the hobby and the disrespect to our heritage. Archaeologists have been caused great anxiety by the thought of devastation of archaeological sites and discoveries which may go unrecorded. Their fears are indeed justified when it is considered that archaeologists excavate a site scientifically, recording and establishing a chronology for each feature, layer by layer on the site. An unqualified excavator is therefore disturbing these layers and denying valuable information to archaeologists and the rest of the country who share the knowledge which can be discovered. If the treasure hunter is interested in ancient history and wishes to participate in the excavation of ancient sites, he should join his local archaeological society. The Department of the Environment compile a comprehensive list of scheduled archaeological sites called *List of Ancient Monuments in England,* and this may be obtained through local libraries or purchased direct from Her Majesty's Stationery Office.

LANDOWNER'S PERMISSION

Unless prior permission has been granted for the treasure hunter to pursue his hobby on specified land, the landowner has the right to prosecute for trespass, and theft for any objects removed from his land. In the event of a treasure trove inquest, he also has a precedent claim to the treasure, or its rewards, if permission was not granted and also if an agreement as to the rights of finds was not previously made.

All land belongs to someone and permission must be obtained by the dump digger, rockhound, metal detector user and prospector alike. The only exception is on a public beach, where the beachcomber and metal detector user may work freely, unless otherwise stated by authorities because of unexploded bombs or other hazards. Little objection also is made to the rockhound who searches beaches, the only limit being that considerable amounts of shingle are not removed from the beach.

Although very necessary, it is nevertheless no easy task to determine ownership of land and it is a difficult subject to approach with any authority. There is absolutely no hard and fast rule to follow when seeking a landowner. The most recent comprehensive survey was conducted over a century ago by the Local Government Board from rate returns and no such extensive survey regarding land ownership has been prepared since. Ownerships which are known and registered at the Land Registry have now come under the Official Secrets Act and are not divulged to the public, and all other such organizations are similarly unrevealing.

The best method of determining ownership usually proves to be in the form of a local enquiry, to the residents of an area, post offices and shops. If, for instance, the metal detector user was seeking the owner of a fairground, he could ask other people who use the land such as fair organizers, who would have obtained permission from the landowner. Similarly, for river sites, fishermen or boatmen may be able to assist. A great deal of land is owned by local councils; and if they are not the owner, they are often helpful in knowing who is. A written request is usually required, including a grid reference of the site, and the treasure hunter's intentions must be made clear to the treasurer of the local council.

When the landowner has been contacted, the request should be made to him or her direct, clearly stating one's intentions and, if done diplomatically and politely, there will probably be no reason for objection. It is strongly advisable, especially if research suggests that a valuable discovery is possible, that an agreement in writing is made with the landowner as to the rights of finds. It is common to agree a fifty-fifty share basis with the landowner in such agreements, though it is merely a matter of personal choice, as is the content of the agreement. All that is really necessary is the written permission to search an agreed area, the rights of finds, and a signature. Its validity in court, if a dispute arises, would warrant a witness signature and more precise details, but it is rare that the landowner would take such action after an agreement has been made.

REPORTING FINDS

Although it is a general rule that the finder of the property retains legal rights to it providing it has been legally acquired, (i.e. landowner's permission has been obtained and an archaeo-

Three commemorative coins which appear to be in mint condition after cleaning. *Left* bronze medallion of the Prince of Wales, 1863; *right* George IV coronation medallion, 1820; *below* George V and Queen Mary coronation medallion, 1911.

Two magnificent silver platters from the Mildenhall treasure trove.

logical site is not in question), other governing factors do however exist.

Firstly, the finder must endeavour to trace the original owner, for it always follows that the previous or true owner has paramount rights. To fulfil his legal responsibility, the finder must take his discovery to the police. It is retained by them, or more commonly by the finder, in a safe place for a stated period. This period varies from one area to another and can be anything up to three months, after which it becomes the property of the finder. If the owner turns up *after* that period, the police are not involved and the matter becomes a civil case.

The question of what justifies a report must of course be left to the discretion of the finder. The type, age and value of the object and the circumstances under which it was found are the deciding factors. Obviously a few coppers are not worthy of action and it would also be unreasonable to assume that the original owner of a 200-year-old coin could be traced. The location of the find, however, must be taken into consideration, for if that coin was found in the street or when searching the grounds of a private house, one's obligation is to report it to the police or landowner. Failure to fulfil this duty for items such as jewellery, money and other valuables where it is reasonable to assume that the owner could be traced, can result in the event being classed as theft.

Landowners' rights and previous owners' rights are the major factors to consider and take precautions against. In very few cases are there other bodies to consider. The legal heirs of the previous owner may have paramount rights to the discovery. It has also been known for a company to put in a claim if a discovery was made by an employee not in his own time, for instance a farm worker who unearths a coin hoard while ploughing.

It is also worth remembering that in the event of a treasure trove inquest or court case, definite favour is granted to the finder if the discovery has been promptly reported in its entirety. The consequences of not doing so immediately, even if the finder is not aware of his legal duty, can be illustrated in the tale of the Mildenhall treasure, discovered in 1946. This famous and priceless treasure contained platters, bowls, goblets, spoons and coins, beautifully and elaborately designed in solid silver and dating back to the Roman period of around AD 407. It was discovered by a farm worker while ploughing, who took it to the farmer. Neither of the men were particularly interested and did not formally declare the discovery. When, however, it became publicly known, a treasure trove inquest followed, for the items were silver and treasure trove laws state that discoveries containing gold or silver must be declared for an inquest. The court's verdict on the Mildenhall treasure was treasure trove, and the finders, because they did not declare the treasure immediately, received only £1,000 each instead of its full value of £1,000,000.

In addition to reporting items which may be claimed by the previous owner, items which are considered of ancient or historical value must also be reported to the police or to a local museum. Any significant discoveries containing even the slightest amount of gold or silver, including coins, plate or bullion must be reported to the county coroner, either via the police or in writing to The Director, British Museum, London WC1B 3DG. It cannot be over-emphasized that the finder should never attempt to clean the item before declaring it.

TREASURE TROVE

A coroner's inquest is held to decide whether a discovery is treasure trove or not. Only items of gold or silver are treasure trove and warrant a treasure trove inquest. If an item is treasure trove, it is the property of the Crown and the finder receives the full market value, but if it is found not to be treasure trove, the finder has the discovery returned to him to use as he will. In each case, it must be remembered that the finder is rewarded only if no one else has a predominant claim.

The decision of whether or not a discovery is treasure trove rests upon whether the item was deliberately concealed by the owner with the intent to retrieve it later, or whether it was simply lost or abandoned. In the latter case the find is not treasure trove, irrespective of its silver and gold content or its value. When it is decided by the court that the find was deliberately concealed with the intent to retrieve it later, it is classed as treasure trove and is therefore the property of the Crown. If the court has reached a verdict of treasure trove, the museum has the right to decide whether or not they wish to keep the item. It is often the case that they only want a proportion of the find or do not want to retain any of it, in which case the treasure is returned to the finder or compensation is given to him for any part retained.

The treasure trove inquest only decides whether the Crown or the finder is the keeper of the treasure and rewards are made to the finder. In the event of a landowner or legal heir making a claim, the matter then becomes a civil one.

In Scotland, treasure trove laws vary in that any object, regardless of its metal, is the property of the Crown if it is considered of ancient or historical importance. A decision as to whether or not the treasure was deliberately buried does not occur. The finder or person with predominant legal rights is rewarded with the market value.

16

THE CORRECT APPROACH

It has been suggested on more than one occasion that treasure hunting with a metal detector should be prohibited because of the abuse it can cause our heritage through damage of archaeological sites and trespass upon land which is then left in an untidy state. The latter has given rise to a great number of public bodies and farm owners banning the use of metal detectors on their land. Although it is only the minority who neglect to fill in holes after digging and fail to request permission from landowners, the effect they have had on what is usually a responsibly followed hobby is widespread and detrimental to all enthusiasts. A request was recently made by the National Farmers' Union asking farmers to refuse access to detector owners who wish to search their land. This was a result of an incident where treasure hunters did not abide by the basic rule of consideration and left the land in a state which was described as 'a mini lunar landscape'. The effects of such conduct are now being experienced by all and farmers who were once open-minded and tolerant of the hobby are now dubiously aware of the possible consequences. Similarly, public places such as parks, commons and some footpaths, display signs or make it clear to metal detector users that their hobby is unwelcome.

Damage which has been done in the past to archaeological sites is the most serious threat to the hobby's existence and is the major point put forward when attempts are made to ban the uncontrolled use of metal detectors. The vast majority of treasure hunters agree wholeheartedly that anyone found searching archaeological sites should be severely dealt with. But for those who do not appreciate this point of view and do not consider the fact that it is illegal as a sufficient deterrent, the main reasons why this law exists are set out below.

Every object in the ground of a scheduled site has a context and if it is not recorded by the correct authorities, a piece of significant evidence is destroyed. This does not only greatly inconvenience archaeologists who, incidentally, do not profit from any recoveries, but the whole community may be denied knowledge of an integral part of our unwritten history. Further cause for concern is given by the fact that discoveries, when made, are not declared or taken to a museum but improperly dealt with through bad cleaning techniques, by selling them or retaining them in private collections while still unidentified or unappreciated.

So what can be done to repair the detector user's reputation and create a harmonious relationship with archaeologists? Some fine examples have been set by treasure hunting clubs and local museums or archaeological societies, which prove that mutual advantages can be found by co-operating with each other. In East Anglia a successful joint venture was accomplished between the newly-established Norfolk and Suffolk Metal Detecting Society and the Norfolk Archaeological Rescue Group. The site was a Roman settlement where the new Caister-on-Sea bypass was proposed to run. When the date for the commencement of building was brought forward, a hasty but accurate search was needed of the site before it was obliterated beneath concrete. Under the directions of the archaeological group, the detector users searched the area in front of earth-moving machinery, while the archaeologists carried out field-walking and excavations. The finds made by metal detector users were recorded in the same way as other archaeological discoveries and included twenty-three Roman coins, Saxon and medieval coins, a hoard of Bronze Age metalwork and many other less significant discoveries.

The venture was a success and it has been said by the Archaeological Rescue Group that another joint venture may well happen again should a similar emergency arise. The event was well controlled and only the members from the detecting society were allowed on site with identification and membership cards to deter unauthorized metal detector users.

Another satisfying and encouraging relationship was forged between the Russel-Cotes Museum in Bournemouth and the local treasure hunters' club. The two parties arranged a meeting and agreed that they would work together to improve relationships. The many treasures which the detector club uncovered thereafter were handed over to the museum in their entirety to be examined by the museum's curator. Many objects were submitted to the coroner for treasure trove inquests and information was gained from the examination of other finds before they were returned to the Bournemouth treasure hunters's club. A joint exercise was also accomplished on a site when results were compared between using detectors and field-walking to collect surface items in the conventional archaeological method. It was discovered that both methods produced efficient results when used together and the detector club also discovered that the exercise was educational in recognizing signs of past civilizations, such as the fragments of pottery found whilst field-walking. The entire venture was carefully watched by the Council for British Archaeology, the Department of the Environment, the Museums Association and the British Association of Numismatic Societies.

It is clear from the above details that efforts to repair reputations and relationships are as well recognized by the authorities as the irresponsible events which have in the past occurred. For this reason, the metal detector user should always consider himself an ambassador for the hobby at all times. Listed below are rules for the correct approach which, if accurately followed, will ensure an enjoyable and uncriticized hobby.

1 Never interfere with archaeological sites or ancient monuments.

2 Study and understand the laws of treasure trove and report any relevant find of gold or silver to the police.

3 Report to the police any item of value which may be reclaimed.

4 Relevant discoveries should be reported to the local museum who will share enthusiasm and assist with the identification and treatment of the object.

5 Request permission before treasure hunting on private land.

6 Never leave a site in an untidy state after use, fill in holes and use methods which require the minimum of disturbance to land when extracting finds.

7 All items such as tin cans and silver paper should not be left on site after finding them. Collect them together and dispose of them in the appropriate place.

8 Abide by the country code. Respect the growth of crops and the presence of animals and ensure that no gates are left open.

INDEX